A
WHISPER
IN THE
WOODS

A

WHISPER

IN THE

WOODS

QUIET ESCAPES
IN A NOISY WORLD

MARTIN WILES

Ambassador International
GREENVILLE, SOUTH CAROLINA & BELFAST, NORTHERN IRELAND

www.ambassador-international.com

A Whisper in the Woods

©2019 by Martin Wiles

ISBN: 978-1-62020-865-6
eISBN: 978-1-62020-886-1

The Holy Bible, New Living Translation, copyright © 1996, 2004, 2015 by Tyndale House Foundation. Used by permission of Tyndale House Publishers, Inc., Carol Stream, Illinois 60188. All rights reserved.

The New King James Version®. Copyright © 1982 by Thomas Nelson. Used by permission. All rights reserved.

THE HOLY BIBLE, NEW INTERNATIONAL VERSION®, NIV® Copyright © 1973, 1978, 1984, 2011 by Biblica, Inc.® Used by permission. All rights reserved worldwide.

Cover Design and Page Layout by Hannah Nichols
eBook Conversion by Anna Riebe Raats

AMBASSADOR INTERNATIONAL
Emerald House
411 University Ridge, Suite B14
Greenville, SC 29601, USA
www.ambassador-international.com

AMBASSADOR BOOKS
The Mount
2 Woodstock Link
Belfast, BT6 8DD, Northern Ireland, UK
www.ambassadormedia.co.uk

The colophon is a trademark of Ambassador, a Christian publishing company.

This book is dedicated to my daughter, Chrissy, and to my middle brother, Jeff. Our years of hiking, camping, and backpacking in the Appalachian Mountains have provided the inspiration for this book. I would also like to thank Latan Roland Murphy for suggesting the title.

BRING ON THE RAIN

Dear brothers and sisters, when troubles of any kind come your way, consider it an opportunity for great joy.

James 1:2

"Into each life some rain must fall."

Henry Wadsworth Longfellow

AND IT DID. BY THE bucketful. My wife and I had headed to the mountains for a few days of camping. Check in wasn't until two p.m., but the camp host said we could come anytime. Knowing the tendency of thunderstorms to crop up around noon in the mountains, we went early.

Gorgeous sunny cool weather greeted us . . . for one hour. No sooner had we erected the tent and put up a tarp than a gully washer marched in. My wife headed for the tent. I stood outside under the tarp. We had chosen the place for our tent based on the electrical box's location. That spot was also the low spot of the campsite.

As the water ran, it puddled several inches deep outside our tent. Soon, I heard my wife say, "We have a problem." I didn't have to ask what. Having no shovel, I used the next best thing, a hammer, to trench the water away from the tent. Then I took the broom and swept away the excess. After the rain stopped, we placed a tarp around that part of the tent to ward off any future puddles, which fortunately never came.

Campers and hikers have a saying about rain: "Rain is not a deterrent, just an inconvenience."

Trials of life are similar. I wouldn't want them to stop coming, just as I wouldn't wish away the rain. Rain brings nutrients and life to God's natural order. Trials also serve important purposes. James told early believers to count is as an opportunity to have joy when they came.

Those who endure trials will receive a crown of life (James 1:12). Trials come to believers and unbelievers alike, but believers face them with a different perspective. We suffer because we stand for Christ and have received Him as our Savior. Persecution, in whatever form it takes, is our badge of courage.

Trials also usher in God's strength (1 Peter 5:10). We have various levels of strength, but none of us can adequately face, endure, and overcome the trial without assistance from God's Spirit. Trials show up God's power in our lives. And nothing can outmatch Him.

So, don't let a little rain spoil your life experience. Better things are ahead—in life and in eternity.

PRAYER: FATHER, THANK YOU FOR sustaining us through the trials of life.

IT'S NOT OKAY

Tell God what you need, and thank him for all he has done. Then you will experience God's peace, which exceeds anything we can understand.

Philippians 4:6b-7a

"NO, IT'S NOT OKAY."

His scream pierced the campground and didn't subside until I got him to Meme. My wife and I hatched a plot: take our two oldest grandsons camping. At the time, they were two and five. Our daughter appreciated the three-day break from motherhood.

Things progressed nicely . . . until we made a trip to the bathroom. On the way back, our two little munchkins laughed and raced. I didn't worry too much that they were in the middle of the road. After all, the campground had only a small number of sites and the name was Lazy J. What could possibly happen?

The youngest of the two—the one we call pig pen or Clumsy Clyde— found a way to fall on the gravel road and skin his knee. He wanted to beat his brother back to the campsite but stepped out of his shoes and tumbled instead.

I couldn't imagine the hurt being serious, so I picked him up and told him he was okay. That's when he screamed loudly enough for the entire campground to hear, "No, it's not okay."

I plopped him into Meme's lap where he had a good cry as she wiped the blood away, applied some antibiotic cream, and sealed the cut with a bandage. Within thirty minutes, he was fast asleep on grandma's lap.

Paul says all we have to do is tell God what we need, while thanking Him for all He has done. Once we've done that, His peace will saturate our entire body, soul, and spirit—if we truly leave whatever it is in His hands and don't take it back to worry over.

Life's trials have a way of knocking us down, scraping our knees, and making us cry. And they tend to do it when we least expect it . . . when we're having fun . . . trying to beat someone else in life's race. Before we know it, we're out of commission and don't know where to turn.

Been there, done that. And instead of running to the Father where I can receive comfort, healing, and peace, I often go to other sources or other people who cannot do what only He can. Unlike my grandson who didn't believe what I said, the heavenly Father truly can make things okay.

When life's not okay, go to the One who can make everything all right.

PRAYER: FATHER, WE COME TO You, believing You can give us peace in all circumstances.

BEAUTY AMIDST
THE CLOUDS

The Lord opened the young man's eyes, and when he looked up, he saw that the hillside around Elisha was filled with horses and chariots of fire.

2 Kings 6:17b

AT FIRST GLANCE, IT APPEARED we'd see nothing.

Balsam Mountain Road. Just off the Blue Ridge Parkway and about half-way between Maggie Valley and Cherokee, North Carolina. A road rising to just over 5,300 feet in elevation. An asphalt road that ends in a loop, but a gravel road that continues another twenty miles to Cherokee. A road that hosts a primitive campground at the end. This was our destination.

As my wife and I turned off the Blue Ridge Parkway and began our ascent, clouds thickened. Passing an old Masonic historical marker, we noticed several elk grazing on the green grass. We stopped to take pictures of animals who didn't seem to mind if we approached them.

The clouds intensified. By the time we reached the campground, seeing the campers and the layout of the campground was difficult. Campers milled about, finishing up breakfast and packing their belongings. We saw only their silhouettes.

Leaving the campground, we trekked down the gravel road toward Cherokee. The clouds remained, but amidst them we observed beauty. Although late in June, several wildflower species still bloomed. Numerous waterfalls flowed over waiting rocks. Birds sang their melodies.

As we struggled to see beauty amidst the clouds, so Elisha's servant also wrestled to see what God was doing. King Aram was angry at Elisha the prophet. Every time the king made plans to attack Israel, God revealed to Elisha the plan, so he could tell the king of Israel. The king of Aram sent a great army to surround the city where Elisha lived. When Elisha's servant saw them, he cried out in fear. Elisha calmed him and asked God to show the servant the beauty amidst the clouds. He did. A hillside filled with chariots of fire. No need to worry.

God is sovereign and always works behind our cloudy skies. We may never know completely what He is up to. He normally gives us only snippets of what He's doing, but we can be sure He is always up to something.

One thing God continually works on is His image in us. He busily forms us into the image of Christ, working to make us more like Him. This requires change. What He asks of us is that we trust Him, submit to Him, and obey Him. When we do, the clouds eventually burn away, and we experience the full beauty of His creation.

Trust God that behind the clouds lies a beauty such as you've never witnessed.

PRAYER: FATHER, WE BELIEVE YOU have our best at heart and are working to complete it in our lives.

THE SPICE OF VARIETY

For in him all things were created: things in heaven and on earth, visible and invisible.

Colossians 1:16 NIV

FOG AND LOW CLOUDS ENVELOPED our destination, giving it the proper atmosphere for the filming of a horror movie.

My wife and I set out for a day trip to an area of North Carolina we had never visited. We planned to visit a primitive campground atop the mountain, perhaps as a future camping spot, and to drive the eighteen-mile gravel road back to the nearest town. Since hot temperatures had dominated our area, we looked forward to the cool temperatures the area boasted about—never rising over seventy degrees.

What greeted us was more eerie—yet more beautiful—than we had imagined. Only a few people camped at the primitive sites which were soaked from the heavy fog and dew. A sign warned us we were entering bear habitat. We didn't know whether this secluded area would be a good spot to take our young grandsons camping or not.

After scouting out the campsite, we began our trek down a nearby gravel road that would take us back to town. Rocks and rain-washed gulleys littered our path. We worried whether or not my wife's small car would make it. But the road said one way. No turning back.

Though most wildflowers had bloomed out, many still shone their colors in this high-elevation area. Only four other people traveled the road with us. Like us, they were in no hurry. We made frequent stops to take pictures of wildflowers, odd-colored mushrooms, waterfalls, and old bridges. We had entered a rain forest, just not a tropical one.

Four hours later—and 800 pictures later—we exited the gravel road safely and made our way to town where we enjoyed a picnic lunch.

According to Paul, Christ created everything we can and cannot see. The beauty of the area we traversed reminded us of the statement's truth. We marveled—and were humbled.

I've learned I can't box God in. Just when I think I have Him figured out, He'll do something different. Traditions can't define or confine Him, nor can my limited understanding. We couldn't understand how the climate could be so radically different when we were only three hours away from our home.

God is sovereign, which comforts me. The beauty of the world He created, and controls, staggers my imagination, as does the fact that He saves all who call on Him.

Learn to enjoy the variety God has placed in the world. Don't try to box Him in by your limited understandings and traditions.

PRAYER: FATHER, THANK YOU FOR giving us a world of variety to experience and enjoy.

DEDICATED TO THE CAUSE

*I don't mean to say that I have already achieved these things or that I have
already reached perfection. But I press on to possess that perfection for which
Christ Jesus first possessed me.*

Philippians 3:12

"THEY ARE JUST TESTING YOUR determination."

My friend said it when I kept losing my bait but not catching the fish. On
the second night of our camping trip with our friends, the husband invited
me to accompany him to the dock for a little fishing. Years had passed since
I'd put a cork in the water, but I agreed to go. Casting the line and watching
the cork bob was difficult. Biting flies nibbled at my legs and neck. Stinging
ants waited for me to lay my hands on the dock railing.

Misery kept me company, but I kept casting the line in various places,
hoping to land a fish. A Johnny-come-lately arrived, cast his line a few times,
and began catching small bream. After landing a few, he left and wished us
good luck. But luck didn't come. We cast in the same spot he did but caught
nothing. My cork bobbled and ducked, but never hung a fish.

My friend wouldn't give up and encouraged me not to either, but after
one hour of bites and stings, I'd had enough. I wound my line and headed for
the campsite—disappointed I hadn't caught a fish, but glad to get away from
my attackers.

Paul didn't give up as easily as I did. God gave him an assignment to take the gospel to the Gentiles—to be a fisher of lost people—and he planned to fish for them until the end, even if it meant his death. And eventually it did.

The believers' cause—our mission, purpose, and plan—to take up where Paul left off by telling others of God's love takes a concerted effort. It also involves a heart issue. My friend helped me by giving me the tools I needed to catch fish, but my heart left the endeavor shortly because of biting insects.

Lone-gospel rangers can't do what Christians together can. Personal trials and persecution from others will attempt to stop our mission or suck the life out of us, but we must press on. Doing so is worth the effort. God gave us an assignment, and we need to keep going regardless of the roadblocks along the way.

God gave Paul the strength to remain dedicated to the cause, and He will do the same for you.

PRAYER: FATHER, KEEP OUR EYES focused on the goal and our feet dedicated to Your purpose for us.

GRABBING THE OPPORTUNITY

*Therefore, whenever we have the opportunity, we should do good to every-
one—especially to those in the family of faith.*

Galatians 6:10

"LET'S GO HELP OUR NEIGHBORS."

A couple whom my wife and I had been long-time friends with invited us to go camping on their maiden journey. The husband had been in a wreck, had undergone surgery, and had missed work for several months. His work-man's compensation settlement gave them enough money to purchase a new camper and a truck to pull it with.

No sooner had we arrived than an elderly couple pulled into the campsite beside us. My friend, more perceptive than I am, noticed they were having trouble setting up their pop-up camper. He walked over, introduced himself, and helped them. The rest of us hung around our campsite.

Over the next several days, my friend visited with the husband, fished with him, and got to know his story. He and his wife once made a good living, only to lose their investments during an economic recession. Now they lived in an apartment and camped often. Neither enjoyed good health, and the husband was legally blind.

The morning my wife and I were scheduled to leave, the couple next door was also scheduled to leave. That's when my friend invited me to go help them break down their camper. Until this point, my camping involved only tents, so I knew nothing about preparing campers for the road. But I was ready to help . . . with instructions from my friend, of course. While helping, I discovered they were a nice couple. Before pulling out, the wife asked for our Facebook names. She wanted to stay connected. I felt as if I'd missed an opportunity to get to know some nice people.

Although I took advantage of the chance to do good, I wouldn't have had my friend not made the suggestion. His initiative embarrassed me when I thought about it later. I wondered how many other opportunities I'd let slip by.

Opportunities abound, but I must put on my spiritual glasses to see them. If I don't see them—or if they're not coming—all I have to do is ask God to send some and then to give me the spiritual eyesight to see them. Opportunities often provide conversation starters which can lead to friendships . . . or even salvation experiences. We never know what God can do with opportunities.

Ask God to send you opportunities to interact with others.

PRAYER: FATHER, SEND US OPPORTUNITIES to do good to those
around us.

THE F.A.L.L.

So she took some of the fruit and ate it. Then she gave some to her husband,
who was with her, and he ate it, too.

Genesis 3:6b

OTHER THAN BEING BITTEN BY a snake or mauled by a bear, I feared it more than anything else.

Hiking in the mountains carries the risk of falling. Roots litter any trail hiked in the Southern Appalachians because forests cover most of the mountains. Stubbing a toe on them is painful. Mixed in with the roots are rocks. On some trails, they cover the entire trail. Twisting an ankle is easy. And steep cliffs bank many of the trails.

Falling when I was young didn't bother me. I never broke a bone. But when I was in my early twenties and fell, I did break a bone. Bones get more brittle as we age—and I had. I've fallen only a couple of times since then and fortunately didn't break anything.

Tripping over a root or rock and then falling could have meant a broken knee or hip or a twisted ankle. Falling off the side of the mountain could mean death. Luckily, I fell only once while hiking and that was on the trail. My pack broke my fall, keeping me from breaking anything else.

Adam and Eve experienced a fall of a different kind. The Bible doesn't use the word, FALL, but their story—and many others throughout the Bible—imply the message. Instead of breaking a limb, they broke something more important: their relationship with God.

19

God didn't want a bunch of robots running around, forced to worship Him, so He gave humans **Freedom**. Although God created us for His pleasure—and because He wanted fellowship with us—He still wanted us to choose to return what He desired.

Freedom involves **Action**. Adam and Eve chose a rebellious act. Although I'm not responsible for their sin, the sin nature they inherited when they disobeyed God has been transferred to every person born since then. While I have good in me, my rebellious bent shows up in various ways. The Bible calls my state **Lost**.

But **Love** led God to pursue me—and everyone else. He did so by allowing His Son to pay for my sin. Then He sent His Spirit to convict me of my need for forgiveness. If I choose to accept it, He grants forgiveness and frees me to be the person He created me to be.

You have fallen, but God wants to pick you up. Why not let Him.

PRAYER: FATHER, WE PRAISE YOU for Your grace and mercy that provides a way for our restoration.

UNTIL THE END

I press on to reach the end of the race and receive the heavenly prize for which God, through Christ Jesus, is calling us.

Philippians 3:14

"NEITHER SNOW NOR RAIN NOR heat nor gloom of night stays these couriers from the swift completion of their appointed rounds."

My dedication to exercise almost parrots a mail person's commitment. In my younger years, I mixed up my exercise regimen by jogging, running, cycling, and walking. Now that I'm older and the joints achier, I stick to walking only.

If I were an inside exerciser, the outside temperature or whatever was falling from the sky wouldn't worry me. But I'm not an inside exerciser. I prefer the outdoors where I can breathe fresh air, gaze at the various patterns of clouds, and listen to the birds. And I walk, regardless. Well . . . almost.

A dedicated hiker or backpacker will not let rain deter them from what they intend to do: hike and backpack. When it comes to exercising, I believe the same and have the notches on my backpack to prove it. As long as lighting isn't popping, sleet or hail isn't falling, or temperatures aren't plunging into the teens, I walk. I enjoy it, know it's good for my health, and realize I could easily find excuses not to if I wasn't determined.

Paul encourages the same kind of perseverance in obeying Christ and living a holy life. He planned to press on until he reached heaven—or met Christ at His second coming.

Persevering to the end takes a determined mindset, such as the one I have about exercising. If I wanted, I could easily find excuses every day not to exercise. Too hot, too cold, raining, tired, too much to do. But I am determined to stay as healthy as possible, so I can enjoy the life God has given me.

On my own, I can't manage the type of perseverance this takes. The courage comes from God who is more than able to supply the determination I need to obey Him in my actions, my words, and the practice of my spiritual disciplines.

Paul knew the benefits of persevering in God's calling on his life. Exercise has benefits. That's why I keep doing it, whether I feel like it or not. I know living as God wants me to live brings peace, assurance, and joy. Doing so may not always be easy—it wasn't for Paul—but it's the best exercise around.

Don't let discouragement, laziness, or other things keep you from persevering for God until the end.

PRAYER: FATHER, GIVE US THE strength we need to follow You
faithfully until the end.

A CONTROLLED BURN

Our God is in the heavens, and he does as he wishes.

Psalm 115:3

WHAT APPEARED UNCONTROLLED, SOMEONE CONTROLLED.

Dusk descended on our campsite as my wife and I enjoyed the third of our four-day camping trip. As she stood before our one-burner stove popping popcorn, she asked, "Is that a fire on the other side of the lake?"

I had seen what she saw, but thought it was lights from houses on the mountainside. It wasn't. I walked to the lakeshore to get a better look. Sure enough, fire ascended and descended up several mountainsides. The site shed a beauty I'd never seen against the dusk-dark sky.

Then a hint of fear grabbed me. I know the damage wildfires can do. Although this burned on the other side of the lake, I wondered if it was headed our way. After taking a few pictures, I started back to our campsite. My wife had good news. A fellow camper reassured her the fire was a controlled burn. He even told her how to know.

Controlled burns burn in a straight line. Wildfires rage in jagged patterns, rising to enormous heights and entering and exiting every nook and cranny. When I looked at the fire, I saw what the fellow camper said about the fire. Our fears disappeared, and we enjoyed looking at what we before had feared.

Sometimes I mistake a controlled burn for a wildfire in other areas. Listening to the news on television or some other media source usually does the trick. Corrupt political leaders. Governments divided and out of control.

Crime escalating. Abuse rising. Fathers leaving. Marriages dissolving. Kids rebelling. World climate rising. The environment changing. But then I read this and other verses that assure me God's doing a controlled burn.

God possesses a perfect and permissive will. Many things that occur in this world and in people's lives fall under His permissive will rather than His perfect will, but even these things He controls and can rework so that good comes from them—such as persecution against Christianity. Instead of stamping out Christianity, persecution has a historical record of causing it to explode.

The same is true in our personal lives. When things appear as out of control as a raging wildfire, they aren't. God is performing a controlled burn. All we must do is cooperate and trust until it burns to the point where He puts it out.

Don't fear the fires that appear out of control. God is executing a controlled burn.

PRAYER: FATHER, WE TRUST YOU to bring and allow things into our lives that will grow us spiritually and form us more into Your image.

RUNNING AWAY

Elijah was afraid and fled for his life.

1 Kings 19:3a

RUNNING AWAY ISN'T ALWAYS A bad thing to do.

My wife and I have faced various financial struggles, one of which led us to run away. Not because we thought we could leave our troubles behind or because we didn't trust God to care for us, but because we needed time to reflect and regroup.

Our go-to spot was the same as always: the mountains. We didn't stay in a fancy hotel, attend shows, or eat at nice restaurants. Rather, we chose a tent overlooking a beautiful lake, and we ate hotdogs, hamburgers, bacon, and country ham instead of steak, seafood, and pork chops.

Three days of running away revived our spirits. We hiked nature trails and marveled at God's creative genius, and we sat in the campsite and enjoyed each other's company. We needed nothing more than still moments before God.

Elijah was a runner, too, but for a different reason. He'd defeated more than 800 false prophets, which didn't please the wicked queen whom they served. Jezebel put a death sentence on Elijah's head, telling him he'd be dead by the next day. In fear, he ran until he landed in a cave where God reassured him, not by miraculous events, but by a still small voice that assured him God still controlled his life events. Elijah's unfounded fear prompted him to run.

Jesus ran, too, but not from an unhealthy fear. He ran deep into a garden to find reassurance and strength to face what lay before Him: the cross. His Father's gentle whispers gave Him courage to die for humanity's sins.

Running away for the right reason gives me a chance to be still before God, a practice that enhances my faith and promotes my spiritual growth. As I walked through nature, God reminded me He controlled our situation. I didn't know how we were going to pay our bills, but somehow anxiety over the how no longer controlled me. God would provide the means. I'm His child, and He has promised to care for my needs.

Running away to a quiet place also helps me hear God. Noise can drown out His still small voice. I need His daily guidance, but I truly need wisdom when things are out of sorts.

When you run away for the right reason, God will reward your flight with peace, assurance, and guidance.

PRAYER: FATHER, WHEN WE RUN, help us to run to You, the author and finisher of our faith.

IN CONTROL

No one can stop him or say to him, "What do you mean by doing these things?"
Daniel 4:35b

WHAT HE THOUGHT HE CONTROLLED, he didn't.

Our foursome—my brother, his girlfriend, my wife, and I—set out to hike a one-mile loop trail where rare wildflowers bloomed from mid-March until early April.

Along the way, we passed a pond that appeared stagnant. My brother remarked that it would be a good place to catch bass. My wife thought it looked like a good place to find snakes. I was more interested in the sign telling the history of the pond.

A farmer dammed the stream to form the pond. Later, he moved. The information didn't tell how long ago the event happened, just what was happening at present. Although the farmer thought he could control the stream, he mistook the power of the stream—and the One who controlled it.

As I walked to the other end of the pond, I noticed the stream exiting and making its way down the mountain. The stream still ran through the pond and was in the process of reclaiming its lost territory. The sign invited visitors to return at a later date to witness the stream's progress. The farmer attempted to change the landscape, but when he left, things began returning to normal.

Daniel said a similar thing about the power of God as the sign said about the strength of the stream. No one can stop God. And questioning why He does something is a waste of time.

Knowing God is in control comforts me. To believe that fate controls things would produce anxiety. I may not understand my circumstances—or why God allows some things to happen in this world or in people's lives—but I can know He's a God of love who acts in the best interests of His people. He promises to work all things together for our good, although His good may look entirely different than what we perceive as good. That's where faith and trust come in.

As the stream controlled the pond—not the other way around—so God controls the events of your life. He loves you and works to form you more into His image so that He can use you to accomplish His work in this world. Don't try to dam up His work in your life. Let Him flow freely and powerfully.

PRAYER: FATHER, WE GIVE YOU complete control to do whatever
You desire in our lives.

MARVEL

Just ask the animals, and they will teach you. Ask the birds of the sky, and they will tell you. Speak to the earth, and it will instruct you.

Job 12:7-8a

"YOU WONDER HOW ALL THIS got in one place," he said.

My brother and his girlfriend were on a three-day camping trip with my wife and me. We chose Devil's Fork State Park in the mountains of Upstate South Carolina. Campsites overlooked beautiful Lake Jocassee, and several hiking trails were in the park and nearby.

The first two days, we did nothing but sit around and soak in the beauty of nature and some relaxation. On the third day, we set out to find wildflowers on the neighboring trails.

The first trail gave us a rare gaze on patches of the Oconee Bell wildflower. We marveled as small white bell-shaped flowers hung from small plants with rounded green leaves. But the second of the three trails we hiked—the Oconee Station historical site—surpassed our dreams. Blooming wildflowers decorated the sides of the trail and the adjoining woods for more than a mile as we made our way to the awaiting waterfall. Many we'd never seen before, flowers that make their appearance only for a short time in early spring, such as purple trillium, Jack-in-the-Pulpit, and May Apple. So many shapes and sizes.

After my brother made his statement at the end of our hikes, his girlfriend motioned to the sky. She didn't have to say a word. We knew what she meant. So, did Job. The earth—and everything on it—speaks of the majesty of the Creator. According to Job, even the afflictions he faced.

When I look at the beauty of the created order, I discover variety yet predictability. These wildflowers will return next year. God created the exact environment they need to grow in this particular area—some in an exact location. God must also love variety or else He would have created everything the same, which would have been simpler.

Gazing on creation presents two options: believe it's an accident or believe someone is behind it. I choose the latter. I also choose to wonder at the God I serve. Greater than all others. Power unlimited. Love unsurpassed. The only proper response is to praise, worship, adore, and trust Him. For everything in life. After all, if He can create such beauty in nature, He can surely take care of us.

Spend some time in nature, and then worship the One who made and controls it all.

PRAYER: FATHER, THE BEAUTY OF Your creation reminds us of
Your love for us.

SECURELY BOUND

I give them eternal life, and they will never perish. No one can snatch them
away from me.

John 10:28

WHAT I NEEDED I DIDN'T have.

Early spring is my favorite time to camp. The nights are cool, which makes for good tent-sleeping weather, but the days can get hot. And they were. Fifty-degree nights turned into eighty-degree days. Since it was early in the season, most of the trees hadn't budded and leafed out. During the heat of the day, our campsite boiled under the sun's rays.

Not wanting a sunburn—but not having a canopy—I wondered how to remedy the situation for my wife and me. I had a tarp but no rope. I improvised. Using guy-lines we didn't use with our tent, we tied them to one end of the tarp. On the other end, we used some thin string I had brought along. But the tarp wasn't high enough to walk under, and the string wouldn't hold.

I improvised again—in a make-do fashion—by duct taping our large umbrella to a hiking stick. This provided just enough shade for my wife and me to lounge under during the hottest part of the day. Duct tape is the gray miracle tape.

What rope, duct tape, and string can't do, Jesus can. He proclaimed the eternal life He gives keeps us alive spiritually forever. And no one or thing can change that situation.

31

Many powerful things exist in this world, but none more powerful than Jesus—and His ability to keep His children securely in His care. Faith connects me to Him, and once I make the decision to make Him my Savior and Lord, He holds me safely in that relationship. I won't want to leave, and no one or no thing can snatch me away.

Nor does staying in this relationship depend on our continual good works or perfect living. Although our sins are forgiven, we're not perfect. Sanctification is a life-long process whereby we grow into holiness by letting Christ teach us how to live for Him and enjoy the abundant life He has in store for us. Mess ups are allowed—and should be expected. But Christ doesn't throw us away when we do.

Our security in Christ is based on what He's done on Calvary's cross, not what we do or don't do on a daily basis.

Take comfort in the fact that nothing can snatch you away from Your Savior.

PRAYER: FATHER, THANK YOU FOR the security we have in our relationship with You.

BE STILL

Be still and know that I am God.

Psalm 46:10a

FINALLY, I FOUND PEACE.

Teaching sixty-plus middle school students can tax anyone's nerves, no matter how proficient a teacher you are. I, and they, anticipated spring break. Their attention spans had diminished more than normal. Things easily distracted them—and me.

And then there was the matter of having resigned one of my two full-time jobs. The people had spoken, silently, and sometimes not so silently. I knew my time to go had come but knowing and doing didn't stop the anxiety.

We needed a getaway—and we had planned one long before I planned to resign. My wife had purchased a large tent. One big enough to accommodate our full-size blow-up mattress along with all the other stuff she planned to take. My brother planned to come along. He needed a break, too.

We arranged for someone to watch the grandboys, and Easter Sunday we headed for our designated campsite in the mountains of Upstate South Carolina. When we pulled into our camping spot, I knew the next few days would relax us. From our spot, we could look out over a large lake. And that's what we did for the few hours after our arrival.

"I'm more relaxed than I've been in a long time," my wife remarked as we parked our bodies in our camp chairs. I shared her opinion, in spite of our

33

tenuous life situation. The first night relaxed us even more. We listened as coyotes howled, Canadian geese honked, and Whippoorwills warbled.

Like the psalmist, our trip taught us once again to remain still and know God is God—regardless of our life situation.

I've learned taking time to stay still before God is essential for my spiritual, emotional, mental, and physical health. But I sometimes get busy and forget. I tend to my physical health, my teaching responsibilities, and my writing details with great accountability—yet sometimes forget to consciously include God in the mix. Often, it takes my wife, or someone else, to remind me to be more aware of God's presence with me and His guidance over my life. As my wife had to on our camping trip. I could have easily found something else to do during spring break, but I needed to be still and know God was God.

When life gets hectic, or even when it's not, be still and let God be God.

PRAYER: FATHER, FORGIVE US FOR the time we forget to be still before You.

THE COVERING

The cherubim spread their wings over the Ark, forming a canopy over the Ark and its carrying poles.

1 Kings 8:7

WITHOUT ANY COVERING, I FEEL exposed, vulnerable, afraid.

When I was a young child, I wanted cover. Even when I stayed with my maternal grandparents in their old farmhouse that had no air conditioning. The summers sizzled, but I craved a sheet to cover at least a part of my body.

At fifty-eight years of age, I still want cover. With a house that has central air and heat, I could adjust the temperature, so I wouldn't need cover, but I have to have it.

And when camping, I want cover. During the hot summer nights, I snuggle in the sleeping bag rather than lay on top completely exposed—as if the sleeping bag would protect me from a bear.

Having cover over my tent is also a good idea, especially if I purchase an inexpensive one that is water resistant rather than water proof. Putting a tarp over the tent keeps the water out should it rain. I've had enough experiences to know what happens when the tent doesn't properly shield water. A soggy sleeping bag, mattress, and clothes aren't enjoyable. Neither is mopping up water from the tent floor. Or feeling the drops splattering against my face while I'm trying to sleep.

King Solomon knew the importance of cover, too. After building the Temple, he had the priests and Levites bring in the various pieces of furniture that would occupy it. Among them was the Ark of the Covenant—the holiest piece that contained the Ten Commandment tablets given to Moses and the piece that represented God's presence. The priests placed it in the Holy of Holies under the wings of two cherubim whose wing span reached from one side of the room to the other. They covered the presence of God.

As His children, God promises to cover us. When life is confusing, disappointing, and depressing, and we can't see which way we need to travel. When the bills are more than the income, and when we don't know how we're going to pay the rent, mortgage, internet, satellite, electricity, or water. When the relationship—or marriage—has gone sour and the door slams never to open again. Or when the children seem out of control, rebellious, and hopeless.

Whatever comes our way, God promises to cover us with wisdom, strength, hope, and peace.

Let God cover you, so you can face whatever comes your way.

PRAYER: FATHER, WE TAKE THE cover You provide so we can endure the trials of life.

FOLLOW THE LEADER

When you hear a sound like marching feet in the tops of the poplar trees, be on the alert! That will be the signal that the LORD is moving ahead of you to strike down the Philistine army.

2 Samuel 5:24

HE LED, AND I FOLLOWED.

My brother loved to lead when we hiked in the mountains. Since he was younger, I sometimes had a hard time keeping up with him, and he'd often have to wait for me to catch up.

Following him led to some interesting circumstances. Once, I followed him to the top of a mountain and watched the path disappear. We had to backtrack. Another time, I shadowed him around a curve and had him almost run over me as he suddenly turned around. A mother bear and her cubs were on the trail. Still another time I trailed him to a yellow jacket's nest in the middle of the trail. And who can forget the time I followed as we stepped over a log, only to find a snake lying on the other side.

One thing that never happened was that we got lost. We always arrived at our destination, sooner or later. One reason is because we had a guidebook which described the trail and gave us markers to look for along the way.

When the Philistines heard of David's anointing as king of Israel, they mobilized their armies to fight against him. With wisdom and faith, David consulted his Leader before attacking them to make sure he did it the correct way. God gave him instructions that led to victory.

Whether I'm aware of it or not, someone is continuously following my lead. I may not know who follows—or why—but they remain seen, and sometimes unseen. My example is important. How I live my life, how I make decisions, what paths I take.

Only as I'm led properly can I lead others. God graciously gives His Holy Spirit to those who choose to follow Him, which in turn gives us the ability to lead others in the right direction. David consulted the Lord before making a decision. How God actually spoke to him, we may not know, but God speaks to us presently through His Word, through the inclination of His Spirit to our spirit, through circumstances, and through others. When we listen, we'll lead others in the right direction, and their lives will be richer for having followed us.

Who is following your lead, and where are you leading them?

PRAYER: FATHER, HELP US LEAD others in directions that take them to a closer walk with You.

REACHING THE GOAL

No, dear brothers and sisters, I have not achieved it, but I focus on this one
thing: Forgetting the past and looking forward to what lies ahead.

Philippians 3:13

OUR GOAL WAS THIRTY-EIGHT MILES and five days away.

Backpacking through thirty-eight miles of wilderness with a twelve-year-old daughter frightened me, but my daughter had decided that's how she wanted to spend her spring vacation from school. We were both new to hiking and backpacking, so I was nervous. I laid out our food and equipment, trying to bear in mind the weight we would carry on our backs.

But preparing our supplies and equipment was only part of the preparation. We had to physically prepare. My daughter ran track and cross country. I knew she could handle the trip. Me on the other hand? I was a little worried. I walked daily, but I was much older and didn't have the upper body strength I thought I needed. Could I carry a fifty-pound pack eight hours a day for five days?

We made the hike—and it was the best hiking experience we ever had—but we had to strip away everything that would slow us down. As I looked over the supplies lying on the living room floor, I selected only what we had to have and did everything possible to lessen the weight of the essentials.

I've set many goals during my lifetime, but the most important one entails what Jesus classified as the greatest commandment: loving Him with my entire being. Examples that spur me on fill the pages of the Bible and

Christian history. But I'll reach the goal only by laying aside the weights that slow me down—among them past sins and failures.

Intentional and unintentional sins litter the past of every believer. We can't undo them, nor can we relive our lives. But we can do what Paul suggested: forget what's behind and strain towards what's ahead. Forgetting is impossible unless we've had brain damage, but we can refuse to dwell on past sins and failures.

When we confess our sins, God wipes the slate clean. He wants us concerned with the present and the future. The past defines us only when we allow it. God defines us by our present and future intentions. The same applies to past failures. The only permanent failure is when we give up and refuse to try again.

Don't let past sins and failures determine who you are today and tomorrow.

PRAYER: FATHER, THANK YOU FOR forgiving our past and giving us a bright future.

STRAINING TO THE END

I press on to reach the end of the race and receive the heavenly prize for which
God, through Christ Jesus, is calling us.

Philippians 3:14

EVERY STEP BROUGHT PAIN, BUT she stepped anyway.

Flat Laurel Creek Trail, near the Blue Ridge Parkway in North Carolina, is appropriately named. Trails over 5,000 feet aren't usually flat, especially in the mountains. This one meanders above 5,200 feet in elevation and maintains an almost level path. And my brother, his girlfriend, my wife, and I planned to hike it.

Although the calendar said November, the weather was mild. We donned our packs and shoes, grabbed our hiking sticks, and headed out. The main creek, along with its tributaries, had swollen from the recent rains. The hike started badly for my wife when she missed a rock crossing Bubbles Creek and landed with both feet in the water. Rocks and mud peppered the trail, making walking difficult.

As we inched along, I observed my wife's face. Pain etched its mark with every step she took. Tears fell, sweat flowed, and feet stumbled, but she kept going. While an easy hike for three of us, it wasn't for her. Degenerative arthritis makes her walking painful—and even more so when the steps are uneven because of rocky terrain.

Due to my wife's tenacity, we made it to the end—just as Paul intended to do. Since God had called and commissioned him on the road to Damascus, he had pressed on with fervor. His goal? Making sure everyone he encountered heard about the saving grace of Jesus Christ.

Jesus said His yoke and burden were easy to carry (Matthew 11:30), but it doesn't always seem that way. The call to serve often involves walking over rocky and uncertain surfaces. What makes the burden of doing so easy—and what gives me the ability to keep pressing on—is the power of God's Spirit in me.

Neither is living the holy lifestyle God commands always convenient. Temptations abound. Ones that would draw me into choices and lifestyles better left alone. Only by God's power can I press on without giving in.

God empowers me to reach the end, and to do so without injury or depletion of energy. My willpower plus His Spirit ensures my pressing on will be rewarded. With prayer, guidance from His Word, accountability partners, wise choices, and encouragement from others, God's children can press on to the end successfully.

Don't let anything or anyone hold you back from straining to your appointed end.

PRAYER: FATHER, WE DESIRE TO make it to the end and hear You say, "Well done, good and faithful servant."

WALKING THE WIDE PATH

You have made a wide path for my feet to keep them from slipping.

Psalm 18:36

WE HAD NO IDEA OUR destination would take us along such a narrow path.

My brother and I aimed for Charlie's Bunion, one of the more attractive spots in the Great Smokey Mountain National Park and so named because it looks like a bunion. But in this case, the bunion perches on the side of a steep mountain. Reaching it requires driving to Newfound Gap—the halfway point between Cherokee, North Carolina, and Gatlinburg, Tennessee—and accessing the Appalachian Trail.

The trail leaving the parking lot at Newfound Gap is wide and pleasant, but conditions rapidly change. Prior to reaching Charlie's Bunion, the trail narrows to a one-way path. Meeting other people requires stepping to the side so they can pass—but the side closest to the mountain. Stepping to the opposite side will send one down a steep mountainside that would likely end in death. Scaling Charlie's Bunion is no safer. We did it anyway. One slip, and we would have fallen from the same mountain.

Hiking in the mountains has carried me along wide and narrow paths. The psalmist said God made a wide path for his travels, and the wide path kept him from slipping. Jesus said something more disturbing about a wide path. Those who travel it see their lives destroyed. The psalmist had another wide path in mind. His led to eternal life and joyful living.

I'd rather ramble along the wide path. And that's the one I've chosen. The path is wide because God prepared it for me. He guides my steps and prepares my future. Walking the wide path keeps me in His will.

Walking the wide path of God's will requires that I obey His commands and serve others with love. But I don't do it grudgingly. God loved me in the past, loves me in the present, and will adore me for eternity. Knowing this, I can't help but demonstrate my appreciation.

Traveling the wide path doesn't mean I won't ever slip. I've fallen on narrow and wide paths. Trials and temptations will try my faith. Sometimes, I'll give in, get bitter, grow discouraged, or fight depression. But this won't be the norm. God is faithful to pick me up, restore my soul, and brighten my outlook on life.

Let God guide you down the wide path where you can experience His love and care—and where you can experience life at its best.

PRAYER: FATHER, TAKE US ALONG the wide path where we can see Your plan for our life materialize.

ENVYING THE HEIGHTS

After sending them home, he went up into the hills by himself to pray. Night fell while he was there alone.

Matthew 14:23

"DAD, CAN YOU WATCH THE boys for a week?"

Although I said yes to my daughter's request, the envy immediately reared its head when she told me why. A work cohort had invited her to fly to Colorado to hike one of the "fourteeners."

"If you have the chance to go, go," I said. "But you won't want to come back."

After reaching the top, she and her friend held up a sign naming the mountain, Mt. Evans—and the height. Envy creeped over me again when she sent a plethora of pictures showing me the views and the trail. I saw that she could see miles into the distance from her height. Though it was nothing but rocks and snow-capped peaks—no trees or shrubbery as our mountains in the East have—there was nothing but beauty.

My wife and I had visited Colorado twice but had never had the opportunity to hike in the mountains. I'm not sure I have the physical fortitude anymore, even if I had the chance. The envy and desire, however, remain, though the financial means to get there and do it escape me.

Something about mountains has always attracted me. From examples in the Old and New Testaments, it appears mountains and God have some special attraction. Loving mountains puts me in good company. More stories

45

about them exist than about the beach. Moses climbed a mountain to receive the Ten Commandments. Abraham scaled one to sacrifice his son of promise—the one millions of descendants were to arrive through. And after feeding the five thousand plus, Jesus traversed one to pray.

Mountains represent the spiritual heights we can reach with God. And physical fortitude and finances have nothing to do with my being able to attain those high places. God requires only mental desire and faith. When I seek His kingdom first—godly things—He will usher me to spiritual heights I've never walked before. I'll view things in a different light. On the heights, peace will reign in my life despite my circumstances. And I'll feel His presence in a way I don't when I choose to settle for less than the peaks.

Ask God to take you to the spiritual heights so you too can experience the life He envisions for you. Don't settle when you can scale the heights.

PRAYER: FATHER, TAKE US TO the spiritual high places where we can dwell with You in abundant living.

FILTERED FOR PURITY

But Daniel was determined not to defile himself by eating the food and wine given to them by the king.

Daniel 1:8a

THE DIFFERENCE BETWEEN USING A water purifier and not using one often means contamination, days off the trail, and painful diarrhea.

I met him on a guided hike. He was the first person I'd ever talked to who had thru-hiked the Appalachian Trail. Thru-hiker is the name given to someone who hikes the entire trail in a single journey. I had questions, and he had answers. But one story rose above the rest: his bout with giardia. Trail angels had left fresh fruit in a stream by one of the AT (Appalachian Trail) shelters. Hunger for more than trail food consumed him. He grabbed the fruit, sunk his teeth into it, and soon regretted his decision. He lost two days of walking, sick from contaminated water.

Never have I drunk from an unfiltered water source. Generally, I use a PUR water filter which guarantees to remove ninety-nine percent of germs. Fortunately, I've never suffered from giardia. Purity is important.

Purity was on Daniel's mind. He was among the first of the exiles to experience deportation to Babylon—a subject of foreign invaders who worshiped pagan gods and read pagan literature. But Daniel stood out, along with his friends Shadrach, Meshach, and Abednego. The king chose them to serve him, but they first needed preparation—which included eating the king's food and drinking his wine. A practice that would defile Daniel according to Jewish laws. He offered a suggestion. He and his friends wanted to try vegetables and water. At the end of ten days, they looked healthier than those eating the king's food.

As believers, our bodies are temples of God's Spirit. He lives there permanently and continuously. What I put into my body affects Him. But it's not the food I eat or the liquids I drink—although they may affect my physical condition. Contamination is more about my thoughts, actions, and words.

Remaining pure means thinking on what is true, just, righteous, noble, kind, uplifting, honorable, and lovely. My thoughts lead to actions, which will be pure or impure depending on what I think on. Actions reflect my character. Through them, people see the real me. And the real me means more than the words I speak.

Nietzsche, the atheistic philosopher who proclaimed God was dead, said of Christians: "I will believe in the Redeemer of the Christians when they act like they are redeemed."

God is holy, makes His children holy in position, and expects us to be pure in our lifestyles. Commit to a pure lifestyle.

PRAYER: FATHER, ENABLE US TO live pure lives as good representatives of the pure God we serve.

STAYING ON THE PATH

My steps have stayed on your path; I have not wavered from following you.

Psalm 17:5

SOME PATHS LEAD NOWHERE.

My brother and I once hiked in Panthertown Valley, just outside of Cashiers, North Carolina. Although a beautiful place, the paths are confusing. The map I purchased at a local hiking store didn't help. The trails through the valley were evident, but they weren't blazed as most places we had hiked were.

Choosing the trail we wanted to hike, we launched out for a day of enjoyment—until we topped a mountain and the trail suddenly ended. Going back the way we came was an option, but a long one. I consulted the map and my compass and selected another way. The way involved bushwhacking down the side of a mountain—and a lot of uncertainty about whether we were going the right way—but we finally made it back to the main path that led out.

Walking on a well-worn path where tree blazes are evident is more comforting. Having a book that describes the trail and what I should observe along the way is an added help. Wavering from the path leads to getting lost—not something I'm interested in doing. Neither was the psalmist. His steps remained on God's path. He had no desire to waver from it.

God's main path leads to heaven. He wants everyone on it. The way to get on it and stay on it is simple: believe Christ paid for my sins, ask for His forgiveness, and obey His commands. Seems simple enough, until I face temptations and trials that attempt to cover the path. But God is faithful and will keep the path in plain view if I remain close to Him.

God's path for my specific circumstances is not always so clear. Following what He wants me to do at any given time—in relationships, employment, career, college, finances—challenges my faith.

While the path to heaven never changes, the path for what God desires we do may change numerous times over our lifetime. Staying on the path takes effort, but God provides the means to do so. By praying—not just repeated words we toss out before we go to sleep—by knowing biblical principles, and by listening to the opinions of spiritually mature friends, we can remain on God's path for us.

God never intends to hide His path from you. Just ask, and He will always make it plain.

PRAYER: FATHER, MAKE YOUR PATH clear for us, and then give us the faith to walk it fearlessly.

ENJOYING TOGETHERNESS

How wonderful and pleasant it is when brothers live together in harmony!

Psalm 133:1

I REDISCOVERED TOGETHERNESS WHILE HIKING in the mountains.

My daughter and I were on a 7.2-mile hike in the mountains outside Clayton, Georgia. As we entered the woods, a sea of ferns covering the mountainside greeted us. I thought, *this is going to be an easy and enjoyable hike.* But the level path suddenly took a sharp drop. Rocks and roots consumed the trail, and rain had made it slippery.

When we reached the bottom, a raging mountain stream—complete with several small waterfalls—welcomed us. We would need the rest. The next mile was a steady uphill climb. The series of up and downhills continued. By the time we were three-fourths of the way through, I was spent. My legs were wobbly, and I wondered whether I was going to make it out. I knew the last mile was uphill. I stopped every twenty yards for a breather and to drink some water.

Fortunately, my daughter kept encouraging me. She patiently waited when I had to stop, and she retrieved my water when I needed it. With her gentle encouragement, we finally walked out of the woods and took a picture of us standing by the entrance sign.

I agree with the psalmist. Life is better when people get along. To be sure, disagreements will occur—they're inevitable. But when they do, we can disagree without having a sour attitude.

Friendships are important, but they don't just happen. We have to intentionally establish them and then nurture them after we do. Good friends will stick with us through the good and bad times. They will encourage us to take the next step when we feel as if we can't.

Enjoying our family is also essential. While we can choose our friends, we cannot choose our family. They come with the territory. Family is like blood: thicker than water. Enjoying our family makes life more pleasant. Families should be there for each other.

But family and friendship can't take the place of time with God. Through Bible study, prayer, and time spent with other believers, we experience the benefits of togetherness with God. And God is there for us when everyone else walks away. He is a friend who sticks closer than the closest relative.

Don't neglect the benefits of togetherness. Life is too short to live it alone.

PRAYER: FATHER, PROMPT US TO make time for others—and especially You.

OUR JOURNEY

For I was born a sinner—yes, from the moment my mother conceived me.

Psalm 51:5

OUR JOURNEY TOOK US THROUGH hardwood forests on a path decorated with rocks, roots, and narrow ledges.

For the first time in twelve years, my daughter and I hiked together. I hoped this would be the beginning of regular hikes again.

Our journey was one we'd taken before. A ten-mile stretch beginning at Whitewater Falls—just across the North Carolina line—and ending at Sloan Bridge. I was older and had more aches and pains than I did the last time we hiked. I warned her my pace might be slower.

Along the way, sweat poured from my body. My feet ached because my shoes were too narrow. My knees throbbed every time we hit a downhill stretch. I occasionally wondered whether I was going to make it, but each time I told myself I could.

After a few short breaks, we arrived at the end. I was glad I could still master mountain hiking, and I was even happier that I had a few hours to journey with my daughter.

Life, too, is a journey, but one the psalmist says begins in sin. The verse doesn't mean his mother was involved in a sinful relationship when she conceived him but that he was born a sinner because she was a sinner. As was her mother and father and their mother and father—and so on back to the time when the first humans decided to disobey God.

Our journey begins with a sinful nature that controls us. Like my hike, this nature takes me over rough and rocky terrain. Unlike my hike, I have no chance of finishing the course successfully without help. My sinful nature dooms me unless someone intervenes.

While the wages of sin are death, the gift of God is eternal life through Jesus Christ. I was able to summon inner fortitude to finish the hike, but I can't do this with my sinful nature. Only Christ can take it away and give me a new nature, and He does so when I admit my sinfulness and plead for His forgiveness.

Because of prior conditioning, I was able to complete the ten-mile hike. I can also complete the journey of life with a hope for eternal life in heaven— but only with Christ's help.

Don't depend on anyone or anything but Christ to help you finish life's journey.

PRAYER: FATHER, THANK YOU FOR the gift of Your Son. May we make our life's journey with Him by our side and in our heart.

SHELTERED

The LORD is a shelter for the oppressed, a refuge in times of trouble.

Psalm 9:9

A SHELTER CAN BE A welcome sight—and it often was for me.

The Appalachian Trail—which extends from Springer Mountain, Georgia, to Mount Katahdin, Maine—is a two thousand plus mile trail dotted with shelters. Some who thru-hike the trail don't even carry a tent but depend on the shelters to protect them from the elements and provide a place to sleep, relax, read, wash clothes, and do other necessary things.

While their construction style varies, each one I've seen was three-sided. Some have fireplaces, but the missing side allows snow and rain to blow in during storms, predators—such as bears and raccoons—to enter at will, and cold and heat to penetrate. Still, sleeping in a shelter is better than lying on the ground during the cold months or in inclement weather.

I've slept in a few of the shelters, and one thing they're not is comfortable. They provide what is necessary, but no creature comforts. While better than nothing, they don't begin to compare with a plush home. After all, those who stay there are backpacking and want to rough it in the wild.

The psalmist didn't find his shelter in a three-sided structure, but in the Lord. He, too, as a lad, was an outside person. He tended sheep and also lived in the wilderness in caves for a time while running from a jealous king. He knew a thing or two about shelters.

As a shelter, God shelters me from sin and its dangers. When I ask, He forgives my sin and restores me to a right relationship with Him. Forgiveness shelters me from the eternal consequences of rejecting Him: hell. He also promises not to let temptations get so intense that I can't walk away from them with His help.

God shelters me through life's disappointments—and they are many. He won't take them all away. They may often have a place in His plan for my life. But He will shelter me from the damaging emotional effects if I turn to Him instead of other things.

God also shelters me through periods of brokenness. When I've lost a job, a child, a spouse, my reputation, my peace, my friends. He gives a peace that surpasses my understanding.

Unlike the Appalachian Trail shelters, God's shelter is fully enclosed, warm, peaceful, and always available. Run there often.

PRAYER: FATHER, THANK YOU FOR being our shelter in our times
of need.

THINKING GOD'S THOUGHTS

When I look at the night sky and see the work of your fingers—the moon and the
stars you set in place—what are mere mortals that you should think about them?

Psalm 8:3-4a

THINKING THE RIGHT THOUGHTS MAKES the difference between happiness and misery.

I've flown in foggy conditions, watched as the pilot took the plane upward, and marveled at how blue the sky was once we got above the clouds. I've also lain on the ground, looked upward, and marveled at the different shapes of the clouds.

I've sat on mountaintops and marveled at how far I could see. Peak after peak, rising into the sky in a seemingly endless range. I've also perched on mountaintops when the clouds were so thick I couldn't see the next peak. But I could see clouds dancing between the peaks and carousing through the valleys.

Nature is a marvel. The psalmist thought so, too. He had been a shepherd and spent many nights looking at the expanse of stars. No city lights existed to interfere with his view. He saw planets he didn't know existed. When he had finished marveling over God's creation, he thought of how small he appeared. What was he that God would even think about him?

But God did think a lot of humanity. So much so that He made them just a little lower than Himself and the angels. He created them in His image.

While we aren't a carbon copy of God, we are more like Him than we are like plants and animals. We can think, reason, feel, and control our actions.

Sin spoiled God's purpose for humanity. He knew we would sin before He created us, but His desire for relationship was worth the risk. He had another plan. Although Satan would think he had won, God's plan was far superior to Satan's. God would allow His only Son to pay our sin debt.

Accepting what Christ has done for me allows me to think God's thoughts about me and leads to a radical change in my emotional conception of myself and others. God's image in me is reborn. God works in my daily affairs to make me more like His Son in actions and words. I am no longer under His condemnation. Christ has set me free. God the Father sees me clothed in His Son's righteousness. He sends His Spirit to continually indwell my life, and I can do all things through Christ who strengthens me.

Think the same thoughts about yourself that God thinks. Doing so will change your life's outlook.

PRAYER: FATHER, MAY OUR THOUGHTS about ourselves mirror Yours and prompt us to be the people You formed us to be.

RECOGNIZING GOD'S VOICE

So he said to Samuel, "Go and lie down again, and if someone calls again, say, 'Speak, LORD, your servant is listening.'"

1 Samuel 3:9

LISTENING TO THE RIGHT VOICES can determine or destroy one's life course.

We were simple country boys who loved to romp through the woods for hours at a time. Times were simpler back then than now. No cell phones. No video games. Only our youth and imaginations. Our parents and grandparents didn't fear someone would kidnap or murder us. My cousin and I were allowed to roam at will as long as we listened for the voice—in our case, our grandmother's car horn. We may have heard other horns in the distance, but this one we recognized. When we heard, we listened and went home.

Young Samuel assisted Eli, the aged priest, in God's work, but he'd never heard God's voice. Messages from God were rare. But to follow God's directive, Samuel had to recognize His voice.

Recognizing God's voice requires training just as young Samuel had to learn to distinguish it from the other voices that commanded his attention. In his time, Samuel may have heard an audible voice. Presently, however, I won't be so fortunate. God speaks through His Spirit to my spirit, so I must learn to hear Him spiritually rather than audibly.

When God speaks, what He says will always agree with His Word. Anything I think I've heard that contradicts God's Word, that comes not from

God but from the enemy of my soul. Just as becoming a good listener takes practice, so learning to listen for and to God also requires the same. Hearing God isn't an automatic process.

Listening to God also demands silence. Silence is difficult in my busy, noisy world. Even doing good things can steal my listening time from God. Jesus left the crowds for a mountaintop meeting with His Father. He often rose early in the morning to speak with His Father. I must be still and know God is God.

Let God teach you the art of recognizing His voice.

PRAYER: LORD JESUS, GIVE US the spiritual wisdom to recognize Your voice so that we might obey Your directives.

LIFE ON A HIGHER PLAIN

I also pray that you will understand the incredible greatness of God's power
for us who believe him.

Ephesians 1:19a

ALMOST WITHOUT EXCEPTION, IT HAPPENED every time we backpacked.

From my late thirties to early forties, my brother, daughter, and I observed a regular routine of backpacking. Several times a year, we would trudge the mountains of the Carolinas, Georgia, and Tennessee. We planned our trips meticulously and looked forward to each one. With one exception—the uphills. Camping spots were almost always in a valley which meant an uphill climb was the first thing we faced the next morning. But the strenuous climbs were always worth it. Reaching the tops provided us with vistas never before witnessed.

Though Paul wasn't describing a hiking trek or a higher plain, he could have been. Obviously, many of the first century believers didn't understand the power they had in Christ. They were dwelling in the valley of satisfaction when there was a higher plain to reach. Understanding the power they had in Christ would propel them to these high peaks.

Living on a higher plain of understanding allows me to use the power God gives to witness. Sharing my faith can be a frightening thing. I never know how people will react, and I sometimes don't know the right words to say. Some may just walk away while others might berate or physically attack me. Though I may fumble my words and risk harm to my person, God's power for me to witness will enable me to overcome both possibilities.

Life on a higher plain entails trusting God's power for life's trials. No temptation will be greater than His power to help me endure and overcome—nor will any terrible situation be so unbearable that He can't walk me through it.

On the higher plain, God also gives me the capacity to touch others in His name. Loving them as I do myself is the second greatest command according to Jesus. God will provide the opportunities and resources if I merely ask.

When living on a higher plain, I'll experience God's ability to help me endure to the end. Jesus said the one who does so will be saved. Life can throw some terrible curves that might tempt us to give up, but the Spirit's power in us is greater than anything the enemy can lob our way.

Don't live in the valley. Live on the higher plain.

PRAYER: FATHER, HELP US REALIZE the power You give that enables us to live on the higher plain.

GOD'S LIGHT

I pray that your hearts will be flooded with light so that you can understand
the confident hope he has given to those he called.

Ephesians 1:18a

MY WORLD CAME CRASHING DOWN, but it was too dark for me to see it.

On one of the first few camping trips my brother, my two children, and I took, we discovered the need for a good tent. I had purchased two small tents—one dome shaped and the other military style. My son and I slept in the military style.

During the night, my tent came tumbling down. I fumbled for my flashlight, and after turning on the light understood why. My son had dislodged one of the poles. Not only had the pole collapsed but the tie-out line had unhooked from the stake. Gratefully, I located the stake, re-attached the line, and re-erected our tent. But only because I had light.

The light Paul wanted early Christians to be flooded with didn't come from a flashlight—or in his time an oil lamp. Rather, it came from understanding the wonderful present and future they had because of God's light of salvation.

When God's light shines into my life, it will enable me to understand Him. While the process of fully understanding God is never complete—His ways and thoughts are higher than mine—knowing Him as my Lord gives me a fuller understanding of who He is. He's not just a far-off deity who really doesn't care about the affairs in my life. He's a close-up friend and Savior who has my best interests at heart.

God's light helps me comprehend His plan. He has a unique plan for each one of His followers. We don't have to aimlessly wander around pondering what we're supposed to do. I can know God's desire for me and join Him in fleshing it out.

God's light shining into my life allows me to see a bright future. Life on earth can be abundant, but life in the future will be more so. Regardless of what I have or don't have on earth, or regardless of how I'm treated, I will be loved for eternity by the One who gave His life for my sins.

When God's light of understanding pours into my life, I'll see the matchless inheritance I've been given. Everything that belongs to God's Son belongs to me. I am a joint heir with Christ.

It's amazing what a little light can do. Are you experiencing God's light?

PRAYER: FATHER, FLOOD OUR HEART with light so we might understand all You have in store for us.

ENDURING LIFE'S THORNS

So to keep me from becoming proud, I was given a thorn in my flesh, a
messenger from Satan to torment me and keep me from becoming proud.

2 Corinthians 12:7b

I HADN'T GARNERED ENOUGH BACKPACKING experience, so my first long haul involved a serious mistake.

When in my late thirties, hiking and backpacking became a love my middle brother and I pursued monthly. But I wanted more. Knowing my daughter would soon be out of school for a week during spring break, I thought what better way to spend the week than hiking a remote section of the Foothills Trail which meanders along the South and North Carolina border.

My mistake was wearing a new pair of boots. Halfway through our first day of hiking, a burning sensation grabbed at the side of my heel. We stopped at the first cool stream of water, so I could investigate. The culprit was a large blister. I cleansed the area, applied antibiotic cream, covered it with a bandage, and moved on. This thorn on my foot required daily care for the remainder of the hike.

Paul was a great apostle, but he had a thorn. Theologians conjecture what it was, but Paul leaves the answer as a mystery. What it was isn't as important as how he responded to it. His actions are noteworthy when dealing with our own thorns.

Paul identified his thorn—not to us, but to himself. I knew what mine was as well. Soldiers in battle must identify the enemy before they can fight the enemy.

Though it's not recorded in Scripture, it's feasible to imagine that Paul asked God why he had the thorn. Asking God a question and questioning God are different. The first is permissible; the second questionable. God may choose to reveal why—or He may keep it a secret. I knew why I had the blister.

Paul asked God to remove the thorn. I would have loved for God to have miraculously healed my blister, but I doubted that would happen until I took the boots off. God didn't take Paul's thorn away either. Paul's thorn had a purpose; my blister did as well.

When God refused to remove Paul's thorn, Paul made peace with his thorn. I did with my blister. I doctored it daily because I knew the risk of infection. Paul was obviously tempted to have a prideful spirit—since he concluded God gave the thorn to keep him humble.

God has a purpose when assigning thorns. If and when you get yours, rather than complaining, ask God what He's attempting to teach you.

PRAYER: FATHER, THOUGH WE DON'T enjoy our thorns, we trust
that You have a purpose in allowing them.

SAFE IN THE SHELTER

Those who live in the shelter of the Most High will find rest in the shadow of the Almighty.

Psalm 91:1

THE SHELTER WAS ONLY A few hundred feet away, but at the moment it may as well have been a mile.

I had grown accustomed to storms while hiking in the mountains. Which is why I started early in the morning, so we could finish before late afternoon when storms were known to arrive. On this day, I was on the Appalachian Trail in northern Georgia with my middle brother, daughter, and son. Our plans were to arrive at our destination around noon, set up camp, and continue hiking for a few more miles.

We reached our destination on time, but as soon as we unloaded, thunder began to march across the mountains. We quickly set up our tents. No sooner had we driven the last stake than powerful pelting rain, sharp peals of lightning, and booming bangs of thunder slithered across the mountains. A trail shelter was only 300 hundred feet away, but we couldn't reach it.

During a brief lull in the lightning and thunder, we made a run for the shelter. Soaked to the skin, we huddled in the crude building for the next four hours, listening as one storm after another tumbled across the mountains.

The psalmist had also discovered a shelter in the God he served—a shelter that provided rest and comfort.

The mountain storms I've encountered were nothing compared to some of the life storms I've experienced. During these times, the shelter of God's protection often seemed close but unreachable. But it only appeared that way. God always has a shelter for my troubled soul. The storm may continue to rage, but I'm protected from harm when I rest in God's sheltering arms.

Just as we had to make an effort to get to the shelter, I, too, must run to the shelter God provides. My effort demonstrates to God that I recognize my need and love for Him—that I've come to understand I can't handle life on my own.

While shelters of various styles dot the length of the Appalachian Trail, God is my ultimate shelter. He manifests Himself in different ways. Sometimes He shelters me through the presence of others.

God's shelters are always close when the storms of life pummel. Run to Him often and find the protection and peace He offers.

PRAYER: FATHER, MAY WE REMEMBER that You are our ultimate shelter in the storms of life.

TRUDGING THROUGH
MUDDY WATERS

When you go through deep waters, I will be with you. When you go through
rivers of difficulty, you will not drown.

Isaiah 43:2a

BEFORE US WAS A WIDE river; behind us were miles of unmarked territory.

Panthertown Valley in North Carolina was the most confusing place I had ever hiked. Numerous trails meandered through hundreds of acres, but none were marked adequately. Maps didn't seem to match the actual outlay of the areas, and several side trails veered off from the main trails, making following the map difficult.

On one hike, my brother, son, and I chose a route we'd not taken before. After hiking several miles, we came to a bulging river. None of us could swim, and we weren't sure we could return the way we had come. While the water wasn't raging, we wondered what would happen if it was deeper than it appeared. My brother decided to be the guinea pig and made it safely across. My son was short; I had to carry him. So, with a child on my back and a hiking staff in my hand, we traversed the cold water and made it safely to the other side.

God's Old Testament people had been through deep and muddy waters more than once. In their history, wave after wave of foreign invaders attacked them and, on several occasions, carried them away as captives. But each time, God delivered them.

Like the nation of Israel, I can recount an entire list of muddy water episodes: rebellious children, dying relatives, financial meltdowns, broken relationships, unemployment, low-paying jobs, abuse, cancer, and physical ailments. And if I haven't faced the muddy waters myself, I've been close to someone who has.

God never gave up on the nation of Israel. He always came to their rescue. He's done the same for me. Just as I couldn't see the bottom of the river we crossed, so I've not been able to see the bottom of the muddy-water episodes I've encountered. But it doesn't matter. I knew the One who allowed me to cross through the waters, and He had a reason for doing so.

The lessons I've learned have resulted in spiritual growth. And God has given me many opportunities to share my lessons with children, teens, and adults. I've also noticed that people traversing muddy-water episodes listen more carefully to someone who has been through the muddy waters themselves.

When God takes you through muddy waters, enjoy the journey and be open to what He's trying to teach you.

PRAYER: FATHER, WE TRUST YOU to guide us through life's muddy waters, believing You will keep us safe and provide something better on the other side.

THE STEPS OF LIFE

The Lord directs the steps of the godly. He delights in every detail of their lives.

Psalm 37:23

SOMETIMES, STEPS CAN LEAD TO uncommon sites.

Porter's Creek Trail is a popular trail in the Great Smokey Mountains National Park. The first mile of the trail is a wide gravel path that passes the remains of several old home sites surrounded by rock walls. In the middle of an odd area, a set of rickety stone stairs leads upward. As I climbed to the top, a small cemetery awaited me—a family cemetery from long ago with mostly illegible headstones.

The psalmist was confident God directed the steps of His followers. Delightfully, He walks along with His children as they traverse the steps of life.

Like the steps leading up to the old cemetery, life's steps can be slippery, uneven, or solid. Had it recently rained, I would have scaled the ancient steps more carefully. Green moss on them would have slowed me down as well. I know what moss on a wet surface can do. Though some may have fallen on these steps, the steps have stood the test of time. Hundreds of years later, they still carry visitors to the old cemetery.

My life's steps will always lead somewhere. When ordered by God, a destination awaits—one that will be brighter than the spot I'm currently in if I let Him lead me all the way through. On the way, the steps may take me through valley experiences, desert depths, and over mountain peaks, but with God guiding I don't have to fear any of those experiences.

Whatever steps God takes me up, I can rest assured He precedes me like a shepherd leading sheep to a greener pasture. The shepherd goes before the sheep and removes poisonous weeds and checks for danger. While climbing the steps, God will walk beside me. If I slip, He will pick me up. If I twist my ankle, He will mend the hurt.

God also designs the steps of life to test my character. Numerous biblical stories and countless testimonies by Christian saints relate it. God's ordered steps for me are never concocted to destroy but to build up and make me stronger spiritually than I've ever been before.

As you climb the steps of life, remember who built them and that they are designed to lead you to a place of stronger character.

PRAYER: FATHER, WE CLIMB YOUR steps for us with confidence that what awaits us at the top will be better than what we've experienced below.

HIDING FROM GOD

What sorrow awaits those who try to hide their plans from the Lord, who do
their evil deeds in the dark!

Isaiah 29:15a

THE FOUR DEER THOUGHT THEY were hidden, but they stood in plain view.

Around eleven a.m., my wife and I started on a hiking trail in the Great Smokey Mountains National Park. We quietly talked about various matters and enjoyed the beauty of nature as we watched evidences of spring pop up all around us. As I glanced up the mountainside, a doe appeared. Then we noticed several yearlings with her. The little family strolled along, nibbling on greenery, obviously thinking they were hidden.

Just as the deer imagined the bare trees concealed them, so many in Isaiah's day thought they could get through life—making their own plans, while ignoring God.

Adam and Eve started this failed attempt to hide from God when they disobeyed God's instructions. When they realized the consequences of their disobedience, they tried to hide. God found them. Then they tried to make excuses. Adam blamed Eve who in turn blamed the serpent.

Since God is everywhere at once, my attempts to hide from Him because I've sinned—or to hide my plans from Him because I don't want His input—are useless. God sees all things at once, me included. But a more important question is why I would want to hide myself or my plans from Him in the first place.

As with Adam and Eve, sin is the normal reason for my attempts at hiding. Adam and Eve played the denial game, then the making excuses game, and finally the blame game. None of their games worked then, and they don't now. I've tried them all.

When I sin or stray from God, attempting to hide isn't the answer. God isn't mean, nor does He sit in heaven waiting for me to mess up. so He can receive joy out of punishing me. He loves with an eternal love and wants to be involved in my life, so I can experience a level of living that can be known only with Him as my guide. Coming out into the open with the details of my life might be frightening—after all, it's a faith thing—but doing so is the only way to live life as He planned for me to do.

Rather than trying to camouflage yourself from God, come out into the open and let Him have full control of your life.

PRAYER: FATHER, WHEN WE ATTEMPT to hide our sin or our plans from You, pull us out into the open through confession and trust.

SPIRIT CLOUDS

The wind blows wherever it pleases. You hear its sound, but you cannot tell
where it comes from or where it is going. So it is with everyone born of the Spirit.

John 3:8

A MUCH-NEEDED VACATION TOOK ME to the mountains of Tennessee.

Along with my wife and another couple, I found myself nestled in a cabin high in the Great Smokey Mountains. Each morning, I sat on the porch, admired the handiwork of my Creator, listened to the birds and turkeys, felt the gentle breezes, and watched the sun rise above the distant peaks.

One morning was different. The sounds were the same, but the sun didn't immediately appear. Rather, dark storm clouds marched through the valleys and hopped over the mountain tops. After dropping their cargo in the form of light rain showers, they gave way to wisps of white dainty clouds that flittered west to east and south to north. As I watched, I thought of God's Spirit.

In Greek, the same word is used for spirit and wind. Though I can see the effects of the wind, I cannot see the wind itself. Nor can I view God's Spirit—only His workings in the lives of people, myself, and in the world.

Like the clouds, God's Spirit is often silent. I hear no audible voice—just a small but effective nudge within my Spirit guiding me in the right direction or to the correct decision. At other times, God's Spirit is loud. I don't have to wonder if it is Him speaking to my spirit. His voice comes through clearly—as clouds that bring vociferous claps of thunder and downpours of rain.

The work of God's Spirit can be obvious. Such as when He brings a change in my life that is evident to others. Or His work can be not so obvious. As when He slowly changes me from the inside out. Changes that take months—or even years—to ripen to maturity.

As witnessing the spirit clouds comforted me on that early morning, so my spirit is calmed by knowing God is always present with me in the form of His Spirit—giving me wisdom and guidance for every decision in life. The clouds went where God sent them, and He never sends them in the wrong direction.

Learn to listen for God's still small Spirit voice. Then act on what He guides you to do.

PRAYER: FATHER, THANK YOU FOR guiding our steps through the still small voice of Your Spirit.

FEAR THE LORD

You must fear the LORD your God and worship him and cling to him.
Deuteronomy 10:20a

BEING AROUND SOMETHING OR SOMEONE I'm scared of is not my favorite adventure.

I have real and perceived fears. My fear was real when bears entered a fellow camper's camp and devoured their food—twice. My son and I were camped in a three-sided shelter a mere fifty feet away. The same bears could have easily walked into our shelter and harmed us.

As a child, my fear of the dark could have been real or imagined. Though Dad was fond of saying there was nothing in the dark that wasn't there in the light, I never believed him. Some dangers are present at night that aren't during the day. But some of my fears associated with darkness were also imagined.

Early in life, Dad taught me to fear the Lord. At the same time, he wanted me to love Him. I don't normally love or choose to be around those I fear. If I fear them, I perceive some sort of danger hangs around them. Seemed like an ironic situation to love and fear God, and I was unsure of how to do both.

The command combines fear, worship, and association. If we usually avoid what we fear—but God wants us to worship and associate with Him—there must be another definition for fear . . . and there is. Fear can involve being afraid of something or someone. Defined in such a manner, I would avoid that person or thing. Fear can also mean to reverence. And this is the definition God has in mind when He tells us to fear Him.

When I reverence God, I will stand in awe of Him. In one sense, I should fear Him. He has life and death power over my existence. With the utterance of one command, my heart would stop and my breath cease. He is sovereign over people and the universe.

Though fear can involve fright, God wants me to love and revere Him. So great was His desire for fellowship with people that He allowed His Son to die for our sins on Calvary. I stand in awe of Him, but I also consider Him my Savior and friend. He has accepted me into His family and invited me to come into His presence as often as I like.

Let your fear of God lead you to Him, not away.

PRAYER: FATHER, WE LOVE YOU for who You are and for what You've done in our behalf.

SWIMMING TO SERVE

When Simon Peter heard that it was the Lord, he put on his tunic (for he had stripped for work), jumped into the water, and headed to shore.

John 21:7b

SERVING GOD SHOULD EVOKE EXCITEMENT.

When I'm excited about an event, I typically don't sleep well the night before. My brother, daughter, and I once planned several camping trips during one year. As the dates approached, excitement over the trip itself, as well as living in the woods for a few days, kept me tossing and turning the night before. Pondering about whether I'd packed everything—as well as thinking about the dangers involved—also kept my eyelids fluttering. Anticipation tends to do this.

Jesus was gone—killed by heartless Roman soldiers and jealous religious leaders. The disciples were alone. Several of them, Peter included, returned to what they knew best: fishing. Suddenly, a man on shore called out and questioned whether their fishing trip had been successful. Hearing of their failure, He instructed them to cast their nets on the boat's opposite side. When they did, the catch was almost more than their boats could handle. John recognized the man as Jesus. Upon hearing this, Peter quickly dressed and swam to shore. Perhaps there was still serving to do after all.

Christ has saved me to serve, but if I see serving as a burden, it will quickly transform into a chore. Chores can be cumbersome and unenjoyable. To serve Christ adequately, I must discover my gifts and then be willing to use them joyfully. Like Peter, I'll have failures and setbacks along the way, but God has always been in the business of another chance. Through experience, examining my personality, and the wise guidance of others, I can cast my gifts. When I'm willing to serve faithfully and with excitement, God will open doors of opportunity for me to swim into.

Serving with excitement entails unconditional love. Those I serve may not serve me back, appreciate my acts, or love me in return. I must remember, however, that my deeds of service are not designed to bring recognition for me but rather shine the light on Christ.

Are you serving God faithfully and with excitement?

PRAYER: FATHER, FOR YOUR GRACE we are thankful. May we use the gifts You have entrusted to us.

LOOKING FOR EVIDENCE

"I won't believe it unless I see the nail wounds in his hands, put my fingers into them, and place my hand into the wound in his side."

John 20:25b

THE EVIDENCE WAS OVERWHELMING. WE followed something we feared.

Panthertown Valley is just outside Cashiers, North Carolina, but if you're looking for a directional sign, you'll be disappointed. My brother and I had directions. Numerous trails run through more than 10,000 acres of protected land, and we planned to hike one of them.

As we made our way along the trail, we noticed scat. Since it was filled with berries, we knew what kind of animal deposited it. Though we enjoyed the scenery, our eyes roamed our surroundings. Every noise caused our hearts to race and our eyes to dance. When we reached the end of the trail, a tree with claw marks greeted us. A bear scratching post. We never saw ole' Smokey, but the evidence convinced us he was near.

Thomas wasn't convinced by the evidence. Jesus had been resurrected from the grave. Women saw Him—as did some of the other disciples, but eyewitness reports weren't enough for Thomas. He wanted to see the marks. So, Jesus showed him. Then Thomas felt ashamed that he'd asked.

The evidence for God's existence seems overwhelming to me—but not all agree. When I look at nature and how natural laws operate according to an unseen plan, I wonder how anyone could doubt, or even deny, the existence of a Higher Being. Theologians disagree over the methods God used to create.

Did He initiate a Big Bang or perhaps use evolution as His process? Or was everything a fiat act of creation out of nothing?

Jesus showed Thomas the evidence he asked for and listened as Thomas shamefully confessed Him as Lord and Savior. He should have believed without the evidence. God won't appear to me and say, "Yes, I exist and created," but He has given me enough evidence to know He does and did.

The evidence at Panthertown Valley convinced me and my brother a bear was in the area—whether we physically saw him with our eyes or not. The universe, along with a still small voice that speaks to my spirit, convinces me God exists, loves me, and wants to be included in my life. What I do with the evidence is up to me.

Evidence for God's existence is overwhelming. Believe He exists and invite Him into your life.

PRAYER: FATHER, WE ACKNOWLEDGE YOU as the Creator and Governor of our universe and our lives.

WHAT A WALK

And Enoch walked with God; and he was not, for God took him.

Genesis 5:24 NKJV

HE WAS THE FIRST TO do what I longed to do . . . but probably never will.

In his book, *Walking with Spring*, Earl Shaffer details his account of being the first person to hike the full length of the Appalachian Trail—a footpath extending more than two thousand miles from Springer Mountain, Georgia, to Mount Katahdin, Maine. The fairly new trail was a mess, not well-attended like today. Nor did he have the modern equipment available presently.

I once dreamed of taking a walk like Earl. Taking six months off from work and living in the wilderness, enjoying God's creation. Although I've hiked numerous sections of the Appalachian Trail from Georgia to Virginia, I've never hiked the entire trail. Now, age and health concerns would prevent me from doing so.

Enoch took a walk of a different variety. He walked with God, and when his time came to leave this earth, God just took him. He didn't have to pass through the scary experience of death. He merely disappeared into God's hands and entered heaven.

To take a walk with God means I must go in the same direction as He does. God is characterized by holiness and righteousness. Walking with Him means I must pursue the same traits. While I can't be purely holy and righteous in practice as He is, I can be in position by accepting what He's allowed

His Son to do on Calvary's cross: pay for my sins. When I accept that act, Jesus' righteousness—which was as pure as God the Father's—is applied to my life.

Walking with God is often taxing as it was for Earl Schaffer as he maneuvered a rough and unkempt trail. But God promises to walk with me, giving me power to make it through the rough spots.

Taking a walk with God requires obedience. Jesus says if I love Him I will obey His commands. Doing so isn't always easy, but He will give me strength to do that as well.

When I walk with God, I can also expect rewards. God gives me the desire to serve Him, the power to obey His commands, and then rewards me for His accomplishments through me. The assurance of His presence and love now and throughout eternity keeps me taking another step.

Walking is good exercise. Take a daily walk with God and reap the benefits.

PRAYER: FATHER, THANK YOU FOR the privilege of walking with You.

PERPLEXED BY TRIALS

Three different times I begged the Lord to take it away. Each time he said,
"My grace is all you need. My power works best in weakness."

2 Corinthians 12:8-9a

"RAIN IS NOT A DETERRENT—JUST an inconvenience."

I'd heard the saying from seasoned hikers. And since I loved to hike, I'd said it a few times myself. Had I postponed hiking trips because there was a chance of rain, I would have stayed home more than I hiked. Unless the forecast was for a total washout, I went ahead with my plans and prepared accordingly.

One such trip was to Tray Mountain in northeastern Georgia. Prior to reaching the summit, hikers reach a mound of rocks with a 360-degree view. But not on this trip. Clouds socked in the valleys and covered the peaks. Occasionally, the stiff winds blew away enough clouds for me to see the surrounding beauty.

My desire to take a hike or to go camping always overruled the inconvenience of rain. I simply prepared for inclement weather by taking a rain coat, a pack cover, and quick-drying clothes. Rain didn't perplex me. In fact, I learned to expect it when hiking in the mountains—which by the way, make their own weather.

Perhaps Paul was perplexed by his trial—an unidentified thorn in the flesh. He wouldn't be the first. Old Testament Job—and a host of others—was as well. When living righteously and loving God supremely, it didn't make sense for life to be tough. Shouldn't it have been easy?

God has the power to initiate or allow trials. When He allows them, that means Satan is the instigator. He hopes the trial will make me bitter and frustrated or want to give up and quit. That's never God's intention when He initiates or allows it. He has good intentions—along with the power to turn around Satan's intentions and overrule them for good.

Rather than getting perplexed by trials, I can choose to focus on their positive effects. They can grow me, making me stronger spiritually so I can face life with a different attitude. They can draw out my ingenuity. God doesn't usually automatically fix things, but He will give me wisdom under His power to see the correct course of action. Trials cause me to look at life differently—to examine my priorities. And they also propel me into actions I might not otherwise take.

Instead of being perplexed by your trials, let God show you the positive side effects of them.

PRAYER: FATHER, WHEN WE MOVE through difficult seasons of
life, show us the positive things that can result.

SEEING THE REAL PICTURE

For we walk by faith, not by sight.

2 Corinthians 5:7 NKJV

WE STOOD GAZING ACROSS THE river at what our eyes couldn't believe.

My daughter and I were on an extended backpacking trip. Our third day out, we came to a swinging bridge that crossed Horsepasture River. But as we looked at the other side, we noticed a large tree had fallen across the stairway ascending the neighboring mountain—the mountain we had to climb. Without binoculars to view the situation up close, we had two choices: turn back or move on. We moved on.

An enormous pine had fallen across the steps. What we couldn't see from the other side was that the mess was passable—with a little ingenuity. Since my daughter was only twelve and skinny, she easily passed beneath the tree. I wasn't so fortunate. I removed my pack, hugged the tree tightly, and shimmied over. Had I slid down the tree, I would have also slid down the mountain.

Just as my daughter and I couldn't see the full picture from where we stood on the other side of the river, so I normally can't see all aspects of my life's journey either. Nor could the greatest missionary who ever lived. He said he walked by faith and included all believers in the journey. Faith helps me see that the real picture isn't as frightening up close as it may appear from a distance.

With faith eyes, I can see God has a plan. His plans for me are good. He wants to bless, not harm. His plans have a purpose, and if I'll pursue His plan

I'll live a more abundant life than I could possibly find through power, possessions, or pleasure.

With faith eyes, I'm reminded there's a spiritual warfare taking place. God wants me to enjoy His best while Satan wants me to pursue his plan. The first brings lasting joy and peace while the second brings only temporary satisfaction—along with eternal torment.

With faith eyes, I can see the victory is won. Christ assured the final victory on Calvary's cross. By relying on His Spirit's power, I can win every spiritual battle I encounter.

And with the eyes of faith, I can believe there's a way through every one of life's trials. God has the path mapped out and will point me in the right direction when I ask.

When your way appears blocked by life's obstacles, God can help you see the real picture.

PRAYER: FATHER, HELP US SEE life as it really is—not as it often appears.

TRAVELING WITH FIRM FOOTING

He makes me as surefooted as a deer, enabling me to stand on mountain heights.

Psalm 18:33

WHERE I WALK DETERMINES HOW I travel.

Backpacking in the mountains taught me the art of careful walking. Rocks, roots, and dead leaves made paths uneven and slippery. If I wasn't careful, I would twist my ankle, get my foot caught on a root, or slip on wet leaves. More than once, my feet magically disappeared from under me.

Having to watch my step while hiking made me wish I was like a deer. While visiting our friends in Henderson, Colorado, we traveled to the Rocky Mountain State Park. The mountains are aptly named and peered at us through the car window as we wound around the curves. Suddenly, they were there, and we pulled to the side of the road for a better view. Mountain goats. But they were like deer—surefooted. They scaled the rocky surfaces— never slipping, as I would have.

I doubt the psalmist actually referred to God giving him the ability to climb a mountain without falling, although he was familiar with mountains. The mountains he needed help climbing are similar to mine: financial, spiritual, emotional, relational, educational, and parental. I've discovered life is filled with such mountains. The psalmist scaled them because God sured up his feet.

Slipping on the mountains I climb is inevitable if I don't let God help me scale the heights. Through prayer, meditation on His Word, and wise counsel, God gives me wisdom to know the right step to take. Even when I neglect these things and fall, He's more than happy to pick me up, steady my feet, and nudge me along.

Although I sometimes fall out of neglect, I periodically fall because God lets me. Falls teach me important lessons. I need to pray before I make decisions. When I make decisions that take me out of God's will, He will discipline me because He loves me. Occasionally, God leads me over rocky slippery paths to prepare me for an upcoming assignment.

While it's my responsibility to watch the path I'm traveling, God will give me sure footing, so I can travel it.

Travel your life paths with confidence. God will give you sure footing to walk down each one.

PRAYER: FATHER, WE TRUST YOU to give us the ability to travel each path You lead us down.

WALKING A WIDER PATH

You provide a broad path for my feet, so that my ankles do not give way.

Psalm 18:36 NIV

WIDE PATHS MAKE FOR BETTER walking.

Several types of paths are found in the mountains. Some are so narrow that one misstep can send you pummeling down the mountainside. Others are so wide that several people can walk side by side. But most are medium in width—narrow enough to keep down a crowd but wide enough to make walking less treacherous.

The psalmist was a shepherd and familiar with paths. Broad paths would accommodate him and the sheep without them having to follow him in a single file. But through poetry, the psalmist has more in mind than a literal path.

Life is filled with challenges. What college to attend, which person to marry, which fund to invest in, whether to rent or buy, whether to buy a used or a new vehicle, whether to follow God's plan or my own, whether to have children, how to trust God when life takes a sour turn and makes no logical sense.

In the challenging times, God will broaden my path if I allow Him. He will widen my perspective—which is naturally limited. I can see only what is present now. I can't even see the rest of the day I'm currently living in. But God? He has lived in the future I haven't experienced. He can help me see with more than my physical eyes if I'll seek Him.

God can widen my patience. Challenges tax my patience. Trials push it to the limit. The things I distaste are what God uses to develop patience in my life. And life will be more peaceful when I learn to walk the wide path of patience.

God can widen my faith. As a believer, this is what I live by. Faith is my trust in a God I can't see whom I believe directs my life's path. Through challenges, God builds, develops, and hones my faith.

And God can also widen my endurance. In my own strength, I'll falter under the least turbulent circumstances. With God's help, I can do all things, weather all things, and learn from all things. I don't live this life with my strength, but with the strength of God's Spirit residing in me.

Depend on God to widen whatever path you're walking on. He will never leave or forsake you.

PRAYER: FATHER, WHATEVER PATH LIFE takes us down, we
depend on You to widen it so we won't slip and fall.

LETTING THE WEIGHTS FALL

Therefore, since we are surrounded by such a huge crowd of witnesses to the life of faith, let us strip off every weight that slows us down, especially the sin that so easily trips us up.

Hebrews 12:1a

EVERY SPRING, THOUSANDS MAKE THEIR way to Springer Mountain, Georgia, to begin their trek to Mount Katahdin, Maine.

The percentage of those who finish the Appalachian Trail, however, is low. In fact, many drop out while hiking the access trail to the initial starting point. Those who continue usually find they must discard much of the paraphernalia they thought necessary: heavy tents, clothes, food. Any item that's not absolutely necessary to completing the journey. Otherwise the weight will weigh down the person's physical shape and, in turn, affect their emotional fortitude. Hiking the trail is more mental than physical.

Since the inception of time, thousands of believers have walked the trail to heaven. All who begin finish, but many grow discouraged along the way, leading them to temporarily get off the trail or become emotionally and spiritually drained. Fortunately, they have many cheerleaders. All those who've made it are cheering them on from heaven.

I've never hiked the entire Appalachian Trail, but my daughter and I have completed the Foothills Trail that runs along the South Carolina and North Carolina border—a feat we're both proud of. On one such five-day trek, we discovered we had taken too much. While we didn't discard anything along the way, we determined we'd pack lighter in the future. Heavy packs make walking cumbersome—especially when hiking up steep peaks.

Many things can weigh me down as I attempt to live the Christian life. What they are, I discover through experience. When I've discovered them, I'm wise to not pick them up again and to stay away from anything or anyone who might encourage me to. These weights may be sins or simply innocent things that get in the way of me serving God fully. Either way, they must go if they hinder my spiritual journey. God is perfectly willing to help me put them away; I must simply ask.

Think about what weights are slowing down your spiritual journey. Then, discard them.

PRAYER: FATHER, AT THIS MOMENT, we let any hindering weights fall so we can run well our race for You.

PACK LIGHTLY

Then Jesus said, "Come to me, all of you who are weary and carry heavy burdens, and I will give you rest."

Matthew 11:28

I WORRIED IF I HAD enough, but it was more than I needed.

Our possessions were spread over the living room floor. The things my daughter and I would need for the next five days: sleeping bags, flashlights, food, clothes, cooking equipment, tent, batteries, matches, toiletries. We were heading out on a four-night, five-day backpacking trip.

Although we were somewhat novices when it came to hiking and backpacking, we had been doing it long enough that I thought we could handle five days without any trouble. I was wrong. After carefully placing all the items from the floor into our packs, I weighed each one. Both of our packs weighed more than the recommended weight. Yet, on this trail, there were no re-stocking places along the way, so we'd have to carry everything we would need.

One day on the trail and I knew we had brought along too much. Our backs ached, and my new boots gave me a blister I'd have to nurture the remaining way. Uphills were miserable, downhills a relief. When we reached our camping destination each day around two o'clock, we were exhausted. But we had no options. What we had, we needed. Still, I came to understand the need to pack lightly.

Jesus called those who were weary and carried heavy burdens to come to Him for rest. My daughter and I were both of those adjectives, but Jesus had other burdens in mind. I've carried many of them at various times in my life and known others who have as well. In fact, at any given time, I may be lugging around two or three of them.

The burdens Jesus references are familiar: fear, worry, anxiety, loneliness, debt, addictions, doubt, tiredness, grief, discomfort, bad relationships. Sometimes, others' actions load me down with these burdens, but normally I don't need any help. I pick them up and carry them all by myself.

God doesn't intend for me or anyone to carry these unbearable loads. Jesus said giving them to Him results in rest: emotional, spiritual, and physical. The rest comes from learning to depend on Him, from going deeper spiritually with Him, and from learning to live with contentment regardless of my circumstances.

Don't lug around loads God never intended for you to bear. Give them to Jesus and experience an incomprehensible rest.

PRAYER: FATHER, OUR TENDENCY IS to pack heavily, but we ask You to teach us to pack lightly.

ENJOY THE JOURNEY

For you know that God paid a ransom to save you from the empty life you
inherited from your ancestors. And it was not paid with mere gold or silver,
which lose their value.

1 Peter 1:18

OUR JOURNEYS WERE CAREFULLY PLANNED, each with a destination in mind.

For several years, my middle brother and I hiked monthly somewhere in the mountains, but we enjoyed the journeys in different ways.

For my brother, the journey was about reaching our designated ending point, getting back to the vehicle, and getting home within a reasonable time. I went along with his idea because he was along with me. My idea of the journey was different. Had it been up to me, I would have enjoyed the journey more by not focusing on the destination point—to say we had hiked so many miles or that we had hiked from point A to point B—but on the journey itself. Stopping along the way to enjoy the views, to identify wildflowers and trees, to read some of the area's history.

While our hikes were good exercise—and helped me keep my weight under control—I'm afraid we missed the joy of many journeys because we focused on the exercise or our destination point. I'd love to go back and do them all over again . . . a little slower.

Life is a journey and should be traveled with a sense of God's presence while I'm taking the journey.

Like others, I'm looking forward to my retirement destination. But I don't plan to sit in a rocking chair on the porch or recline in my recliner all day when I do. Being caged in the house for five days with a bout of the flu was enough to let me know I don't plan to sit around when I retire. That's simply the end of one journey. I plan more—but maybe not ones where a boss dictates what I do daily.

Nor do I plan to retire from God's work. Neither does He want me to. God's assignment for me may change numerous times during my lifetime. I'm learning to enjoy the journey of each assignment rather than looking for a completion point.

God has many lessons to teach during our various journeys. Don't work simply to get through with the task and miss the important and beautiful things along the way.

PRAYER: FATHER, TEACH US TO enjoy the journeys, as well as what
You teach us along the way.

TAKING THE RIGHT PATH

Lead me in the right path, O Lord, or my enemies will conquer me. Make your
way plain for me to follow.

Psalm 5:8

LIFE HAS MANY PATHS, AND some are not clearly marked.

Miles from nowhere, my daughter and I plodded along with nothing but a guidebook, supplies, and hiking sticks. Several days alone in the woods can be a frightening experience.

The more terrifying part was walking for miles without seeing a white blaze. According to the guidebook, one should be able to stand beside one blaze and see the next one. Rarely did that occur. One day, we went miles without seeing a blaze. Add to this that many side trails led off in various directions, and I sweated over whether we were on the right path.

The only thing that made me relatively sure we were going in the right direction was reading the descriptions in the guidebook. The writer described things a hiker should see along the way. And even though we didn't see the blazes, we saw the other things.

The psalmist pleaded for God to lead him along the right path. If God didn't lead him—or if God did but he didn't listen—the consequences might be severe. He also wanted God to make the path plain, unlike some sections of the path my daughter and I travelled.

Since life has many paths—represented by the numerous decisions I have to make—knowing the right one is essential. Otherwise, I might find myself in unnecessary debt, broken relationships, jail, or any other number of unpleasant situations.

Taking the right path is possible when I consult the guidebook. God calls it His Word. We call it the Bible. Any direction I need is found there. Life progresses, scientists discover, and technology advances, but the principles of God's Word never get outdated. They are good for all time.

Prayer keeps me on the right path. Through prayer, I petition God to give me full understanding of His Word, to help me know how to apply it to daily situations, and to guide others in the same path I'm traveling. Prayer helps the guidebook come alive in daily life.

Communing with other believers is also wise. Passing other hikers who were coming from the direction we were going assured us we were traveling in the right direction—even if we had not seen any blazes. There is strength and comfort in numbers.

Don't guess about whether or not you're on the right path. You can know.

PRAYER: FATHER, LEAD US ALONG the right paths in life so we'll
end up where You want us to be.

MORNING BY MORNING

*Listen to my voice in the morning, L*ORD*. Each morning I bring my requests to*
you and wait expectantly.

Psalm 5:3

I COME FROM A FAMILY of morning lovers.

My paternal grandfather was a morning man. He had to be. His job demanded it. He delivered milk in bottles to people's homes. People wanted their milk when they got up in the morning. If it wasn't there, they would complain or take their business elsewhere.

My maternal grandfather also loved the morning, but not because his job required it. He was a farmer and could have gotten up any time he chose, but he got up early to enjoy nature. With cigarette in hand, he retired to the front porch, listened to the birds, and waited for the sun to cap the tops of the tall pines across the field. It was his morning tradition.

Dad also rose early. But for a different reason than his dad. Morning was his time to pray and read the Bible. It was a tradition he maintained until he died. And for many years, I followed suit. When my children were small, morning was the only quiet time in the house—except for later in the evening. Evening didn't work for me. My mind shuts down after dark.

The psalmist was a morning person. He had no alarm clock to awaken him, but he rose early and took his requests to the Lord.

While God doesn't dictate morning as the time we must come to Him, He does have a lot to say through those who followed Him about the advantages of coming to Him in the morning. Jesus Himself did.

Our minds are fresher in the morning. I may still be sleepy, but the clutter of the day hasn't cluttered my mind yet. Some function better at night, but the advantages of the morning are weighty. Quiet reigns, which allows me to focus.

When I approach God in the morning, the day is before me. I've not made any mistakes or decisions yet. The potential, however, is there. What day doesn't involve decisions, temptations, or potential mistakes? Coming to God in the morning allows me to petition Him for guidance, strength, and wisdom.

Regardless of what time I come before God, coming consistently is important. Just as regular communication with others stabilizes friendships, so spending time each day with God cements our relationship with Him.

Morning by morning—or whenever is good for you—spend time with God.

PRAYER: FATHER, DRAW US TO You daily to receive the spiritual nourishment needed to face each day.

WILDERNESS THINKING

*Normally it takes only eleven days to travel from Mount Sinai to Kadesh-barnea
... But forty years after the Israelites left Egypt ... Moses addressed the people.*

Deuteronomy 1:2-3a

WHAT SHOULD HAVE BEEN A four-hour drive took us twice as long . . . but it was our fault.

My wife and I—along with another couple—once rented a cabin in the Tennessee mountains. We had no specific plans other than to visit antique shops and thrift stores. After four days of doing what we love, we headed home . . . a short four-hour drive. Yet, it was eight hours later before we finally pulled into our driveway. We didn't get lost, nor was traffic the culprit. Love for flea markets was. We chose to stop at several on the way home.

The Israelite's trip was lengthier for a different reason. What should have been a brief journey from Egyptian slavery to Promise Land freedom, took forty years.

Wilderness thinking limits God due to our disobedience. When Moses sent the original spies into the Promised Land before the Israelites attempted to enter, they returned with a discouraging report. The land was beautiful, but the people were fearsome, and the cities were gated. No hope for entrance . . . no chance to conquer. So, God taught them a forty-year lesson about the importance of obedience.

Wilderness thinking limits me. The entire generation who left Egypt perished in the wilderness. Only their children and two of the original spies were allowed to enjoy the blessings of the Promised Land. Sin and self-effac-ing limits God because I limit what I perceive He can do in and through me.

Negativity is also typical of wilderness thinking. The spies' report was negative, as was the attitude of almost the entire million people who escaped Egypt. God could never satisfy them very long with the food, water, shelter, or shoes He provided. Negativity keeps me—and anyone associated with me—in the wilderness.

Are you in the wilderness of your mind? Let God lift you up and bring you out of your self-imposed desert.

PRAYER: GOD OF DELIVERANCE, BRING us out of our wildernesses thinking into Your green pastures of optimism.

PERSPECTIVE FROM
THE MOUNTAIN

Then they stood on each side of Moses, holding up his hands. So his hands
held steady until sunset.

Exodus 17:12b

HINDSIGHT IS TWENTY-TWENTY. HEIGHT ALSO has the potential to change perspective.

I sat on the jagged summit of Tray Mountain in northern Georgia, United States. Three hundred sixty-degree views are normally enjoyed from this peak . . . but weren't on this day. The cool winds of winter had settled in along with clouds from a stubborn cold front. What should have afforded me panoramic views beyond description now only delivered clouds, wind, and a brief view of what might have been.

Height usually delivers a distinctive angle. It did for Moses. As long as he stood on the mountain with his arms held high, the Israelites won the battle against their enemies. When his arms grew tired and threatened to languish at his side, his brother and a close friend held them up. From his vantage point, Moses witnessed a victory.

Normally, God's perspective varies from mine. He's like a Moses on the mountain while I'm more akin to a Joshua fighting in the valley. I suppose as Joshua and the Israelite army fought the long hard battle they looked up to the mountain and saw Moses' raised arms and gained hope for victory. When I take on the mind of Christ by purposefully aligning my plans and goals with His, I ,too, can count on victory. Mountain perspective takes into account the valleys but isn't destroyed emotionally by them.

Perspective affects my actions and emotions. The Israelites could have given up or fought unskillfully. Seeing Moses spurred them on. Knowing that God sees the sunshine above the clouds I may be currently viewing brings happiness, contentment, and a measure of peace. These in turn prompt me to keep on keeping on.

Viewing life from God's perspective rather than my own gives me hope. God's guidance is trustworthy because His love is unconditional. There will be times when it appears I might be losing. In those periods, I look to the mountain and remember no weapon formed against me shall prosper.

Ask God to give you the proper perspective when things are cloudy.

PRAYER: GOD OF POWER, WE look to You for the correct perspective on our lives.

MESHING PERSONALITIES IN RELATIONSHIPS

Thank you for making me so wonderfully complex! Your workmanship is marvelous—how well I know it.

Psalm 139:14

WHAT ATTRACTS US TO SOMEONE else can be the very point of conflict thereafter.

I'm an introvert. I thrive on alone time. I can sit on a mountain peak for hours at a time and feel energized. Or on the back porch of a mountain cabin overlooking the protruding peaks and undulating valleys. No company needed. Curling up in either of these two places or in my recliner at home is perfectly satisfying. No sound required.

My wife, on the other hand, is an extrovert. She thrives on people and noise. She's a social butterfly. Of course, we complement each other. She makes up for what I lack in social skills, but on the other hand, I remind her of the importance of down time. We knew each other's personalities before we married. But if we aren't vigilant, what attracted us to each other can become a source of conflict.

Meshing personalities begins with recognizing different personalities exist. God made all people wonderfully complex with different body styles and personality types. Extrovert versus introvert. Sensor versus intuitive. Thinker versus feeler. Judger versus perceiver.

Only when I understand the language and actions of a person's personality—whether it's my spouse, child, peer, or work partner—can I adequately communicate with them, work with them, appreciate them, and enjoy their company. Knowing the enemy—or in this case the other person's personality characteristics—is half the battle.

Rather than personality types causing conflicts, they can add spice to relationships, and life in general. Had God created us identically, life would be boring. The traits that attract me to others may be the exact things that lead to conflict later if I'm not watchful. Appreciating and complementing the personalities of others and the differences they display, however, will lead to unity and a richer life.

When others' differences seem to get in the way, remember God made us as we are. Seek peace, not conflict.

> PRAYER: GOD OF WONDER AND beauty, help us use our differences to make this world a better place.

SHARE THE LOAD

Carry each other's burdens, and in this way you will fulfill the law of Christ.
Galatians 6:2 NIV

WITH MORE THAN TWO THOUSAND miles to walk, he chose carefully what to put in his backpack.

World War II was over, and Earl Shaffer needed to walk it out of his system. He chose the Appalachian (or Government) Trail to do so. At the time, the trail began at Oglethorpe, Georgia, and extended to Mount Katahdin, Maine. Since most of the men had been away fighting in the war, the trail had fallen into disrepair, making the journey more challenging.

Earl's motto was "Carry as little as possible but choose that little with care." And he did. He carried a survival tent, poncho, rain hat, knife, axe, sewing kit, snake-bite kit, cook kit, clothing, and a week's worth of food. Even though he chose the bare minimum to put in his pack, he still felt loaded down.

Because of Earl's training and determination—and because he chose with care what he carried—he became the first person to thru-hike the Appalachian Trail.

My backpacking experience has taught me how important it is to choose my load with care. My first extended backpacking trip with my daughter revealed I hadn't learned Earl's wisdom. My pack weighed in at fifty pounds and my daughter's at thirty-five. Though we had fun, we also experienced misery because of unnecessary weight. Our loads slowed us down and gave us a backache.

What Paul states in this verse makes common sense. Any burden shared is lighter. Jesus said the load of obeying Him was easy, so if following Him is causing me misery I must be doing something wrong.

Burdens are cumbersome when I carry the wrong things in my life's pack. They might include bitterness, unforgiveness, anger, immorality, depression, frustration, hurt, or lies. When I carry unhealthy emotions, actions, or relationships, my soul aches. Nor does anyone want to help me bear them.

My helping others and their helping me also makes the load lighter. Many people helped Earl along the way, making his journey more bearable and ensuring his success. People who took him to get food and supplies. People who gave him a place to stay out of the inclement mountain weather. Giving others permission to hold me accountable, helping others bear their life loads, and depending on God for strength are all vital.

Don't try to do life alone. Share the load.

PRAYER: FATHER, MOTIVATE US TO carry each other's loads and, most of all, to depend on You for strength to do so.

For more information about
Martin Wiles
and
A Whisper in the Woods
please visit:

www.lovelinesfromgod.com
www.facebook.com/martinwilesgreenwoodsc
www.twitter.com/linesfromgod
www.instagram.com/lovelinesfromgod
www.linkedin.com/in/martin-wiles-5a55b14a

For more information about
AMBASSADOR INTERNATIONAL
please visit:

www.ambassador-international.com
@AmbassadorIntl
www.facebook.com/AmbassadorIntl

If you enjoyed this book, please consider leaving us a review on
Amazon, Goodreads, or our website.

More Inspirational Nonfiction from Ambassador International

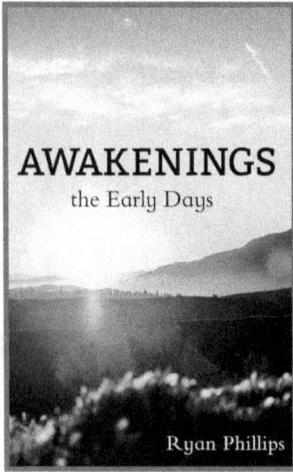

AWAKENINGS
the Early Days

Ryan Phillips

Awakenings is a collection of Ryan Phillips' responses to the truth of God's Word that came during a season of solitude and reflection in the remote and beautiful hills of Laupahoehoe, Hawaii, as he awoke every morning and had time to reflect on the Word and listen to the Holy Spirit.

Awakenings

by Ryan Phillips

I Can Stand on Mountains assumes that each of the mountains mentioned in the Bible has a unique meaning and significance. They are more than topographical features; they are spiritual icons for us to understand.

I Can Stand On Mountains

byDan Manningham

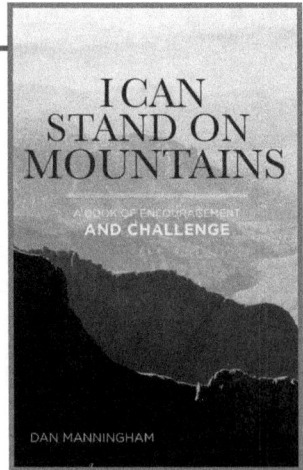

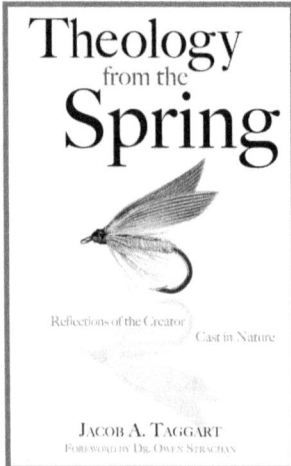

I CAN
STAND ON
MOUNTAINS

A BOOK OF ENCOURAGEMENT
AND CHALLENGE

DAN MANNINGHAM

Theology
from the
Spring

Reflections of the Creator
Cast in Nature

JACOB A. TAGGART
FOREWORD BY DR. OWEN STRACHAN

Theology from the Spring uses beautiful vistas gleaned from freshwater springs and fly fishing motifs that converge with rich theological applications. Fly fishing and freshwater springs are a tonic for the soul, each flowing forth with primal truths.

Theology from the Spring

by Jacob A. Taggart

www.ingramcontent.com/pod-product-compliance
Lightning Source LLC
LaVergne TN
LVHW051602080426
835510LV00020B/3099